India's **Environment** *Policy:*

From Protection to Sustainability

Abhay Kumar

BlueRose ONE
Stories Matter
New Delhi • London

BLUEROSE PUBLISHERS
India | U.K.

For permissions requests or inquiries regarding this publication, please contact:

BLUEROSE PUBLISHERS
www.BlueRoseONE.com
info@bluerosepublishers.com
+91 8882 898 898
+4407342408967

ISBN: 978-93-7825-842-8

Cover design: Ajay Dhyani
Typesetting: Sagar

First Edition: May 2026

To My Father and Late Mother

Preface

India's environmental policy stands at a defining crossroads in the twenty-first century. As a nation balancing rapid economic growth, demographic pressures, and aspirations for global leadership, India faces the complex challenge of preserving its rich ecological heritage while pursuing inclusive development. Various reports indicate, India is facing overlapping environmental crises- climate extremes, pollution, water stress, waste, biodiversity loss, etc. These crises underscore that environmental degradation is now systemic and cross-sectoral, not limited to forests or air. Climate variability plus water stress and soil-health issues are threatening rural livelihoods and food security. Air pollution remains a severe health burden across urban and rural areas – reducing life expectancy and increasing disease burdens. Groundwater extraction is rising; many districts now rely on deep aquifers. Heavy metals pollution is detected in rivers in numerous monitoring sites. Water scarcity and contamination are increasing threats to health, agriculture and livelihoods. Municipal solid waste generation remains huge; a significant portion remains uncollected or dumped. E-waste and plastic waste are growing rapidly. Many States underperform across multiple indicators – infrastructure for sewage, waste treatment, pollution control remains inadequate.

Rapid industrialization, urbanization, and economic growth have lifted millions out of poverty, yet they have also strained air, water, land, and biodiversity to breaking points in many regions. As one of the world's fastest-growing economies–and home to extraordinary biological, cultural, and climatic diversity–India faces the dual challenge of sustaining economic development while safeguarding its natural capital. This book on India's environmental policies emerges from that tension: between a rich legacy of ecological wisdom and the urgent need for modern, science-based, and equity-oriented governance. Over the decades, the country has built a robust and evolving environmental governance architecture that spans constitutional mandates, legislative frameworks, institutions at multiple levels, judicial activism, scientific expertise, community participation, market mechanisms, and an expanding network of international commitments. This book seeks to illuminate that journey—its achievements, innovations, and the continuing challenges that shape India's pursuit of a sustainable future.

India's environmental consciousness is deeply rooted in civilizational traditions that revere rivers, forests, biodiversity, and nature as integral to human well-being. However, modern environmental policy began taking shape in the early 1970s when environmental degradation—manifested in deforestation, water pollution, industrial accidents, and loss of biodiversity—became evident. The 1972 Stockholm Conference on the Human Environment marked a turning point, prompting India to establish the National Council for Environmental Planning and Coordination, and later, in 1985, the Ministry of Environment and Forests, which is now, Ministry of Environment Forest and Climate Change (MoEFCC). Over the years, India enacted a series of landmark laws including the Water (Prevention and Control of Pollution) Act, 1974; Air (Prevention and Control of Pollution) Act, 1981; Forest Conservation Act, 1980; Environmental (Protection) Act, 1986, etc. which became the umbrella legislation for environmental governance.

A defining feature of India's environmental framework is the wide array of institutions that together shape policy, monitoring, enforcement, and implementation. At the centre is the MoEFCC, responsible for policy formulation, environmental clearances, conservation of forests and wildlife, climate action, coastal zone regulation, and the administration of major environmental laws. Its attached institutions—the Central Pollution Control Board (CPCB),

Indian Council of Forestry Research and Education (ICFRE), Botanical Survey of India (BSI), Forest Survey of India (FSI), etc.– contribute scientific assessments, environmental monitoring, and technical expertise. Equally important are the State Pollution Control Boards (SPCBs) and Pollution Control Committees, which monitor industrial compliance, enforce pollution norms, grant consents, and implement waste-management rules. Urban local bodies and panchayats have increasing responsibilities under the Solid Waste Management Rules, Plastic Waste Management Rules, and obligations related to water bodies, sewage treatment, and open waste burning.

Beyond the Ministry of Environment, several sectoral Ministries/Departments of Government of India also play decisive roles. The Ministry of Power supports energy efficiency and renewable energy integration, while the Ministry of New and Renewable Energy (MNRE) has spearheaded India's transformation into one of the world's fastest-growing renewable energy economies. The Ministry of Housing and Urban Affairs shapes urban environmental sustainability through missions such as Swachh Bharat (Urban), AMRUT, Smart Cities Mission, and policies on water supply, sewage, and waste. The Ministry of Agriculture influences soil health, agro-ecology, pesticide regulation, and sustainable farming. The Ministry of Jal Shakti oversees Swachh Bharat (Rural), water conservation, groundwater regulation, river rejuvenation, and watershed programmes. The Ministry of Commerce and Industry affects environmental policy through export standards, green industrialization, and trade compliance with global environmental norms such as the EU's Carbon Border Adjustment Mechanism (CBAM). India's environmental policy has continually evolved to address emerging challenges. The introduction of Environmental Impact Assessment (EIA) procedures in 1994 and its subsequent updates institutionalized the requirement that major infrastructure and industrial projects assess and mitigate environmental impacts. Conservation strategies expanded with the Wildlife Protection Act, National Biodiversity Act, establishment of protected areas, tiger reserves, and community-based conservation programmes.

Indian judiciary has also played a uniquely transformative role in environmental protection. The Supreme Court's expansive interpretation of Article 21 established the right to a clean and healthy environment as a fundamental right. Through public interest litigation (PIL), the courts have addressed issues ranging from air pollution in Delhi to forest conservation, river protection, and hazardous waste regulation. The establishment of the National Green Tribunal (NGT) in 2010 created a specialized forum for swift and expert adjudication of environmental cases, significantly shaping compliance, accountability, and environmental jurisprudence.

India's environmental programmes also reflect strong community engagement. Joint Forest Management, community forest rights under the Forest Rights Act, Watershed development programmes, and biodiversity management committees strengthen decentralized stewardship of natural resources. Civil society organizations, research institutions, and citizen movements–from cleaning lakes to protecting forests–form an integral part of environmental governance.

Over the last few decades, India has embraced market-based instruments and economic reforms for environmental protection. These include green tax, pollution charges, emission trading schemes for particulate matter in States like Gujarat and Maharashtra, renewable purchase obligations, green cess, carbon credits, and green budgeting. The Perform, Achieve and Trade (PAT) scheme for energy efficiency has become a global example of an innovative, industry-focused market mechanism. India's environmental policy now extends far beyond regulation. It also includes renewable energy incentives; monitoring systems driven by digital technologies;

community-based conservation initiatives; and the integration of sustainability into industrial policy, urban planning, agriculture, and infrastructure development. International cooperation—through the Paris Agreement, Convention on Biological Diversity, UNFCCC negotiations, and India-led platforms like the International Solar Alliance—has positioned India not only as a participant but a leader in global environmental diplomacy.

Recent, MoEFCC Annual Reports, reflects a clear shift towards integrated, multi-pronged environmental governance – combining climate mitigation (renewables, emissions intensity reduction), conservation (forests, wetlands, biodiversity), sustainable lifestyles & civil-society participation (Mission LiFE, Green Credits), regulatory reform (faster environmental clearance), and waste/pollution management under circular economy frameworks. It underscores that the government is increasingly aligning national development goals with global climate commitments (under the Paris Agreement), while also recognizing the importance of grassroots-level behavioural change – through lifestyle, waste reduction, planting, conservation – as central to environmental sustainability. At the same time – the report makes clear that the path ahead is long: achieving durable ecological health, sustainable urbanization, waste-free growth, climate resilience and biodiversity protection will require stronger implementation, better data transparency, and deeper public engagement.

Despite these rich institutional and policy landscape, India faces enormous environmental challenges. Rapid urbanization has outpaced planning, leading to severe air pollution, waste-management crises, declining green cover, and water scarcity in many cities. Industrial growth continues to exert pressure on rivers, soil, and ecosystems. Agriculture faces soil degradation, groundwater depletion, and increasing vulnerability to climate extremes. Biodiversity loss, deforestation for infrastructure, land-use change, and habitat fragmentation threaten ecological balance. Climate change amplifies these challenges, manifesting in heatwaves, floods, droughts, glacier retreat, and coastal vulnerability.

Governance challenges persist in form of weak enforcement, inadequate coordination among agencies, limited technical capacity at State and local levels, delays in environmental clearance processes, and insufficient public awareness. Financial constraints, especially for pollution control and waste-management infrastructure, impede progress. Informal sectors—particularly in waste recycling—need formal recognition and safer practices. Balancing development needs with ecological protection remains a continuous struggle.

Yet India's determination to advance environmental sustainability is evident. Commitments to achieve net-zero emissions by 2070, expand renewable energy capacity to 500 GW by 2030, create green hydrogen ecosystems, adopt circular economy principles, restore degraded land, and build climate-resilient infrastructure demonstrate a bold national vision. India's leadership in international platforms, including the International Solar Alliance and Coalition for Disaster Resilient Infrastructure, reflects a global commitment to sustainable development.

This book offers a comprehensive examination of India's environmental policy—its origins, institutions, laws, programmes, milestones, and future directions. It weaves together historical evolution, institutional frameworks, policy instruments, judicial contributions, and emerging challenges such as climate adaptation, urban resilience, water stress, pollution, circular economy transitions, and sustainable finance. As India navigates an era defined by climate uncertainty and ecological stress, the insights offered here will be invaluable to students, policymakers, researchers, and citizens. Understanding the strengths and shortcomings of India's environmental governance is essential to shaping a future where economic progress and environmental stewardship are not competing goals but mutually reinforcing pillars of national prosperity.

This book seeks to present a comprehensive, analytical, and contemporary account of how India has approached this challenge through its environmental policies, regulatory institutions, and governance frameworks. In an era defined by climate uncertainty, ecological risks, and the urgency of sustainable development, the study of India's environmental policy is more than an academic pursuit—it is a necessary guide for shaping the pathways toward a resilient and equitable future. This book is a valuable resource for anyone seeking to understand not only how India responds to environmental challenges today, but how it envisions a greener, more secure tomorrow. The need for such a work is more urgent than ever. Issues such as air and water pollution, climate change, extreme weather events, waste mismanagement, biodiversity loss, and pressures on forests and coasts have moved from the margins to the centre of public discourse. Yet environmental policy in India is not confined to one ministry or one law; it is an intricate network of Acts, rules, missions, schemes, and inter-institutional mechanisms that span diverse sectors—from energy, industry, agriculture, and transport to water, forests, and urban development. Understanding this interconnected framework is essential for students, practitioners, policymakers, researchers, and citizens who seek clarity on both the achievements and the persistent challenges in India's environmental governance.

This book attempts to bridge that gap. It traces the evolution of environmental policy from the early conservation ethos of independent India to the detailed legislative architecture that emerged after the 1970s. It examines the role of key institutions such as the Ministry of Environment, Forest and Climate Change; the Central and State Pollution Control Boards; NITI Aayog; the National Green Tribunal; and a wide array of sectoral ministries whose policies increasingly shape environmental outcomes. It analyses major schemes—from Project Tiger and Compensatory Afforestation Fund Management and Planning Authority (CAMPA) to the National Clean Air Programme, Green India Mission, and circular economy initiatives—highlighting both successes and shortcomings. Equally important, it explores how global environmental negotiations, scientific assessments, judicial interventions, civil society movements, and market-based instruments have influenced India's policy trajectory.

This book is not merely descriptive; it is analytical and forward-looking. It seeks to help readers appreciate the strengths of India's environmental policy system, identify enduring gaps in implementation, and understand the opportunities for transformation in the coming decades. As India aspires to build a sustainable, inclusive, and climate-resilient future, a deeper knowledge of its environmental governance framework becomes indispensable. I earnestly hope this will contribute meaningfully to that journey—informing debate, guiding policy thinking, and encouraging a new generation of scholars and practitioners committed to environmental stewardship. This provides a systematic and critical examination of India's environmental policy landscape—its historical foundations, institutional arrangements, legal instruments, programmes, and future pathways. By integrating analysis of domestic policies with global influences, judicial developments, community engagement, and market mechanisms, it offers a comprehensive understanding of how India is responding to environmental challenges. In an era marked by ecological uncertainty and climate risk, such understanding is essential for shaping a development model in which economic advancement and environmental protection reinforce, rather than undermine, each other.

Content

Chapter 1:

Evolution of India's Environment Policy

India's environmental policy from 1947 to 1972 lacked a comprehensive framework, relying instead on inherited colonial-era laws and scattered post-independence measures focused on industrial effluents, water quality, and resource management. This period emphasized rapid industrialization, sidelining ecological concerns. Several colonial period Acts addressed specific environmental issues vaguely and indirectly. For example, Easement Act, 1882 was applied to address nuisance issues such as pollution affecting property rights and Indian Penal Code, 1860 (Sections 268, 277, 278, 290) for penalizing public nuisance, fouling of water bodies, and air pollution. Factories Act, 1881 (later 1948) was applied for waste disposal arrangements and it also empowered States to regulate effluents; River Boards Act, 1956 enabled regulation of inter-State rivers to prevent pollution, Mines and Minerals (Regulation and Development) Act, 1957 controlled mining impacts on land and water and State-level laws, like Maharashtra's Water Pollution Prevention Act of 1969, supplemented these efforts. No central environmental Agency existed before 1972, as issues like sewage and sanitation fell under separate Ministries without coordination. The constitution originally lacked explicit environment concerns and entered the policy agenda mainly through public health, flood control, and soil conservation. The Constitution's lists assigned related subjects (e.g., public health, forests) mainly to States, leading to limited national oversight.

The Stockholm conference of 1972 catalyzed a paradigm shift, leading India to create environmental institutions and laws such as the National Council for Environment Policy and Planning (later the Ministry of Environment and Forest) and the Wildlife Protection Act, 1972. The 42nd Constitutional amendment Act in 1976 inserted article 48A (State duty to protect environment) and 51A (Citizen' duty), embedding environmental protection into Directive Principles and Fundamental Duties. Environmental protection in India received strong constitutional backing through Fundamental Rights and Fundamental Duties. The Constitution provides the foundation through Article 48A, directing the State to protect and improve the environment, and Article 51A(g), assigning citizens a duty to safeguard forests, rivers, and wildlife. These provisions established environment protection as both a State obligation and a citizen responsibility. The Seventh Schedule distributes environmental responsibilities across Union, State, and Concurrent Lists, with forests and wildlife moved to the Concurrent List by the 42nd Amendment. The 73rd and 74th Amendments empowers Panchayats and Municipalities in local environmental management. It empowers Panchayats and Municipalities to handle local environmental issues such as waste management, water supply, sanitation, land use and planning and has strengthened decentralized environmental governance.

Background for the Enactment of the Water (Prevention and Control of Pollution) Act, 1974

By the late 1960s and early 1970s, rapid industrialization, urbanization, and population growth had led to severe pollution of rivers, lakes, and groundwater. Major river systems such as the Ganga, Yamuna, Damodar, and Hooghly were receiving untreated industrial effluents and municipal sewage. Existing laws like the Indian Penal Code and local municipal laws were inadequate to address large-scale and scientific pollution control. Further, prior to

1974, India completely lacked a Central law dealing exclusively with water and air pollution related issues. Regulatory mechanisms were fragmented across sectors, focusing more on water use and development rather than pollution prevention. There were no specialized pollution control institutions or uniform standards applicable across States. Another important factor was the transboundary nature of rivers and pollution and this usually required Central government intervention. India's participation in the United Nations Conference on the Human Environment (Stockholm, 1972) was a major catalyst. The Conference emphasized environmental protection as integral to development and encouraged nations to create institutional frameworks for pollution control. India's commitment at Stockholm directly shaped the enactment of the Water Act. In sum, the Water Act, 1974 emerged from ecological stress, institutional vacuum, constitutional innovation, and global environmental consciousness, laying the foundation of modern pollution control law in India.

The Water (Prevention and Control of Pollution) Act, 1974

The Water (Prevention and Control of Pollution) Act, 1974, is India's first comprehensive law to prevent, control, and reduce water pollution. Its primary aim is to maintain or restore the wholesomeness of water in rivers, lakes, wells, and other water bodies. The Act established the Central Pollution Control Board (CPCB) and State Pollution Control Boards (SPCBs) as statutory authorities responsible for monitoring water quality, regulating effluent discharge, and enforcing legal standards. It introduced a mandatory Consent to Establish and Consent to Operate mechanism for industries and sewage-generating units. The Act empowers SPCBs to inspect facilities, take samples, set effluent standards, order treatment systems, and prosecute violators. It prohibits the discharge of pollutants into water bodies without prior approval. Penalties include imprisonment and fines, though enforcement remains a challenge. The Water Act laid the foundation for India's modern environmental regulatory system and significantly strengthened institutional water governance.

The Water (Prevention & Control of Pollution) Cess Act, 1977

The Water (Prevention & Control of Pollution) Cess Act, 1977, was enacted to provide a dedicated financial mechanism for implementing the Water Act, 1974. It imposed a cess on water consumed by specified industries and local authorities, based on the quantity and purpose of use, such as processing, cooling, or domestic needs. The cess aimed to promote water conservation and raise funds for the Central and State Pollution Control Boards. A key feature was the rebate system, offering up to 25%–70% reduction to industries that installed pollution-control equipment and complied with effluent standards, thereby incentivizing cleaner operations. SPCBs assessed and collected the cess using water-meter readings, and funds supported monitoring, laboratories, and enforcement. The Act was repealed in 2017 to streamline taxation under Goods and Services Tax (GST), shifting pollution-control financing to consent fees, environmental compensation, and government grants.

Dimension	Water (Prevention & Control of Pollution) Act, 1974	Water (Prevention & Control of Pollution) Cess Act, 1977
Purpose	To prevent, control, and abate water pollution; ensure water quality.	To levy a cess on water consumption to fund CPCB/SPCBs activities.
Nature of Law	Regulatory and prohibitory environmental legislation.	Fiscal/resource-mobilization legislation.
Core Focus	Pollution prevention, effluent standards, industrial regulation.	Water conservation and financial support for pollution control.
Scope	Applies to industries, local bodies, individuals	Applies to specified industries and local

	affecting water bodies.	authorities using water.
Key Mechanism	Consent to Establish (CTE), Consent to Operate (CTO), effluent standards, monitoring.	Levy of water cess based on quantity and purpose of consumption.
Institutions Created	Establishes CPCB and SPCBs with defined powers.	Does not create new body; uses CPCB/SPCBs for assessment and collection.
Type of Instrument	Regulatory: standards, sampling, inspections, penalties.	Economic: cess, metering, rebates for pollution-control compliance.
Enforcement Tools	Legal penalties, closure orders, prosecution, fines, imprisonment.	Financial penalties for non-payment or false declaration.
Incentives	Compliance ensures operational permission	Up to 25%–70% rebate for industries with pollution-control equipment.
Revenue Use	Not revenue-focused; operational functions funded by government and fees.	Revenue dedicated to strengthening CPCB/SPCBs labs, monitoring, enforcement.
Overlap/Integration	It provides regulatory backbone.	Supports the Water Act by providing money for enforcement.
Current Status	Still in force.	Repealed in 2017 after introduction of GST.

Air (Prevention and Control of Pollution) Act, 1981

Air (Prevention and Control of Pollution) Act, 1981, was enacted to fulfil India's commitments under the Stockholm Conference and to address rising industrial and urban air pollution. Its main aim was to prevent, control, and abate air pollution and maintain acceptable air quality standards. The Act empowers the Central Pollution Control Board (CPCB) and State Pollution Control Boards (SPCBs) to monitor air quality, regulate emissions, and enforce compliance. States may declare any region an Air Pollution Control Area, within which industries must obtain Consent to Establish and Consent to Operate before emitting pollutants. The Act authorizes SPCBs to set emission standards, inspect facilities, sample emissions, order closure or restriction of non-compliant industries, and prohibit the use of polluting fuels or equipment. Although it strengthened institutional regulation, enforcement challenges persist due to weak penalties, limited control over vehicular emissions, and inadequate capacity of SPCBs.

The Forest (Conservation) Act, 1980

Prior to its enactment, forests were largely under the control of State governments, leading to large-scale diversion of forest land for agriculture, mining, industry, dams, and infrastructure without adequate scrutiny. The Act marked a decisive shift from a State-centric and revenue-oriented forest management system to a nationally regulated conservation framework. It is one of India's most significant environmental legislations, enacted to curb the rapid depletion of forest cover and ensure the conservation of forests as a national asset.

The primary objective of the Forest Conservation Act is to restrict and regulate the diversion of forest land for non-forest purposes. Under the Act, no State government or authority can de-reserve forest land, use forest land for non-forest purposes, assign forest land to private entities, or clear naturally grown trees without the prior approval of the Central Government. This centralized approval mechanism was introduced to bring uniformity, transparency, and scientific scrutiny in decisions affecting forests across the country. The Act thus aims to balance developmental needs with ecological sustainability.

Another important objective of the Act is to check deforestation and maintain ecological stability. Forests play a crucial role in regulating climate, conserving biodiversity, maintaining hydrological cycles, preventing soil erosion, and supporting livelihoods of forest-dependent communities. By subjecting forest diversion proposals to environmental appraisal and compensatory measures, the Act seeks to ensure that forest loss is minimized and mitigated wherever it is unavoidable.

The relevance of the Forest Conservation Act has increased significantly in the context of rapid economic growth, infrastructure expansion, and climate change. Since its implementation, the Act has contributed to a notable reduction in the rate of deforestation and has strengthened institutional oversight of forest governance. The introduction of compensatory afforestation, the creation of the Compensatory Afforestation Fund Management and Planning Authority (CAMPA), and the requirement for forest clearance procedures have reinforced accountability in forest land diversion.

The Act is also relevant from a constitutional and policy perspective. It complements Article 48A of the Constitution, which directs the State to protect and improve the environment and safeguard forests and wildlife, and Article 51A(g), which imposes a fundamental duty on citizens to protect the natural environment. Judicial interpretations have further strengthened the Act, notably through landmark Supreme Court judgments such as the T.N. Godavarman Thirumulpad case, which expanded the definition of forests and ensured stricter enforcement of conservation principles. Despite criticisms regarding procedural delays and constraints on development projects, the Forest Conservation Act remains a cornerstone of India's environmental governance. It does not prohibit development but mandates that development involving forests occurs only after due ecological consideration and mitigation. In an era of climate commitments, biodiversity loss, and sustainable development goals, the Act continues to be highly relevant in ensuring that India's forests are conserved for ecological security, intergenerational equity, and long-term national interest.

Environment Protection Act (EPA), 1986

Background: On the night of 2–3 December 1984, a large volume of methyl isocyanate gas escaped from the Union Carbide pesticide plant in Bhopal, Madhya Pradesh, spreading over densely populated areas around the factory. Thousands died within hours and in the following weeks, and estimates of total deaths over time range into the tens of thousands, with hundreds of thousands exposed and many suffering long-term health impacts. At the time of the disaster, India had sectoral pollution laws like the Water Act 1974 and Air Act 1981, but there was no umbrella legislation giving the central government broad, direct powers over industrial environmental risks. In December 1985, Oleum gas leaked from Shriram Food and Fertilizer Industries in Delhi, causing the serious health issues to several people in capital. The factory was located in a densely populated area, raising serious concerns about industrial safety. The Bhopal gas leak and Oleum gas leak in Delhi exposed a major regulatory vacuum in India and was a key catalyst for the enactment of the Environment (Protection) Act (EPA) in 1986, which created a comprehensive framework empowering the Union government to regulate and control industrial pollution.

In this background, Parliament enacted the Environment (Protection) Act, 1986, notified in March and brought into force on 19 November 1986. The Act was passed under Article 253 of the Constitution to give effect to international environmental commitments (notably Stockholm 1972) but it is widely described in Indian legal and policy literature as a direct response to, and compelled by, the Bhopal gas tragedy. The EPA 1986 gives the central government wide powers to "protect and improve the environment," including setting standards for emissions and discharge, regulating and closing industries, and delegating powers to specialized authorities. Post-Bhopal reforms also included stricter rules on hazardous processes and chemicals under the EPA framework and related rules, aiming to prevent industrial disasters and strengthen criminal liability and penalties for non-compliance. Policy and legal commentary consistently treat Bhopal as a turning point that accelerated the move from fragmented pollution control to an integrated environmental protection statute.

The Environment (Protection) Act, 1986, often called the umbrella legislation, is one of India's most comprehensive environmental laws. It integrates air, water, soil, and hazardous waste management under one framework. The Act empowers the Central Government to take all necessary measures to prevent, control, and mitigate environmental pollution. Pollution includes the presence of any substance that may harm the environment, human beings, or other living creatures. The Act provides broad definitions covering air, water, land, and their interrelationships. The Act authorizes the central government to make rules, set environmental quality standards, regulate industrial locations, and control emissions or discharges. It empowers the authorities to prescribe: emission standards, effluent discharge limits, noise limits, handling of hazardous substances, procedures for accident prevention and notification. It allows authorities to inspect industries, examine equipment, and take samples for analysis. Authorities can inspect industries, examine equipment, and take samples for analysis and allows enforcement actions against polluting entities. It also facilitated coordination among central and State authorities by providing legal backing for notifications like: Coastal Regulation Zone (CRZ) rules, Environmental Impact Assessment (EIA) notification and Waste management rules (e-waste, plastic, biomedical, etc.). Its wide powers allow the government to restrict industrial operations in ecologically sensitive areas. However, critics note that implementation remains weak and power is overly centralized. Overall, the Act serves as a crucial legislative tool for environmental governance in India.

Major Provisions of the EPA, 1986

Provision	Description
Section 3	It deals with power of Central government. It authorizes the Central government to take all measures for environmental protection, set quality standards, regulate industrial locations, and issue notifications (e.g., EIA, CRZ).
Section 4	It pertains to appointment of officers. It allows the government to appoint officers for environmental protection and delegate powers to them.
Section 5	It empowers the government to issue binding directions, including closure, prohibition, or regulation of industries.
Section 6	It enables the government to frame rules on emission/effluent limits, handling of hazardous substances, noise levels, and accident prevention.
Section 7	It prohibits discharge of pollutants beyond prescribed standards.
Section 8	It mandates safe handling, storage, and transport of hazardous chemicals.
Section 9	It requires industries to report accidental discharges and take preventive steps.
Section 10	It authorizes officials to inspect sites, equipment, and environmental compliance.
Section 11	It provides procedures for collecting and analysing environmental samples.
Section 12	It recognizes environmental laboratories and analysts for official testing.
Section 13	It empowers the government to appoint/notify analysts for pollution testing.
Section 14	It specifies that analyst reports serve as legal evidence in court.
Section 15	It provides for imprisonment up to 5 years and fines for violations, with enhanced penalties for continuing offences.
Section 16	It holds management of company liable for environmental violations.

EPA gives sweeping powers to the Central Government with minimal checks, leaving State governments with limited autonomy despite being key implementers. Despite strong legal powers, enforcement is weak due to shortage of staff, outdated monitoring systems, and inadequate capacity of SPCBs. EPA does not embed participatory rights; public involvement appears only through subordinate rules like EIA, which themselves have been criticized for dilution. Punishments under the Act—often limited to imprisonment or small fines—are insufficient compared to the scale of industrial pollution and economic gains from violations. Most substantive provisions exist in rules and notifications, not in the Act itself. This allows governments to easily amend safeguards without parliamentary scrutiny. Further, EPA overlaps with Water Act, Air Act, Forest Conservation Act, and municipal laws, causing regulatory confusion and delays.

The Environment Protection Act, 1986, is a powerful but under-utilized law. While it provides a strong legal foundation for environmental governance, its impact is limited by weak enforcement, regulatory dilution, centralized control, and inadequate participation mechanisms. Strengthening institutional capacity, updating penalties, increasing transparency, and integrating community rights are essential to make the Act truly effective.

A brief comparison table between EPA 1986, Air Act 1981 and Water Act 1974 is tabulated below:

Feature	EPA 1986	Air Act 1981	Water Act 1974
Scope	Air, Water, Land and Hazardous substances	Air only	Water only
Authority	Central Govt	CPCB & SPCB	CPCB & SPCB
Nature	Umbrella law	Sectoral	Sectoral
Rules	EIA, CRZ, Waste rules	Air quality norms	Effluent norms
Penalties	Strongest	Moderate	Moderate
Flexibility	Very high	Limited	Limited

Article 21 of Constitution and its interpretation by Supreme Court and key judicial pronouncements

Pollution free environment is indispensable for the inhabitants of this planet. The Supreme Court of India taking cognizance of this fact, in its judicial creativity has accorded the right to live in a pollution free environment the status of a fundamental right under Article 21 of the Constitution of India. Article 21 of the Constitution of India guarantees that "No person shall be deprived of his life or personal liberty except according to procedure established by law." Initially, Article 21 was interpreted narrowly, limited to protection against arbitrary deprivation of life and liberty. However, from the late 1970s onwards, the Supreme Court adopted a liberal and dynamic interpretation, recognizing that the right to life is not merely animal existence but includes the right to live with human dignity. A degraded environment was seen as a direct threat to life, health, and well-being. The Supreme Court has also expanded Article 21 (right to life) to include the right to a clean and healthy environment, forming the basis of India's environmental jurisprudence. Modern principles—precautionary principle, polluter-pays, inter-generational equity were also reinforced through judicial activism under Article 21. The Supreme Court, in M.C. Mehta v. Kamal Nath (1997), held that the government is a trustee of natural resources and must protect them for public use and clearly established Public Trust Doctrine. Polluter Pays Principle was recognized in the Vellore Citizens Welfare Forum case (1996), this principle mandates that the polluter bears the cost of environmental damage. Precautionary Principle was recognized by the Supreme Court to take preventive measures even if there is no scientific certainty about environmental harm. Sustainable Development was underlined by the Court by consistently upholding the balance between environmental protection and economic growth. And Absolute Liability was established in the Oleum Gas Leak Case, this doctrine holds industries strictly liable for environmental harm, regardless of negligence. Through judicial activism and purposive interpretation, the Supreme Court (SC) has liberally expanded the scope of Article 21 to include the right to a clean, healthy and sustainable environment. This interpretation has transformed Article 21 into the cornerstone of India's environmental jurisprudence. Some of the key judicial pronouncements are:

- Maneka Gandhi v. Union of India (1978): Though not an environmental case, this judgment expanded Article 21 by introducing the doctrine of substantive due process, enabling courts to assess the fairness and reasonableness of laws affecting life and liberty. This laid the foundation for environmental rights under Article 21.
- Rural Litigation and Entitlement Kendra v. State of Uttar Pradesh (1985): Known as the Dehradun Quarrying Case, the Court ordered the closure of limestone quarries causing ecological degradation. It recognised that environmental destruction violates the right to life of affected communities.
- M.C. Mehta v. Union of India (1986 onwards): In a series of landmark cases, the Court firmly established that pollution-free water and air are integral to Article 21. In the Oleum Gas Leak case, the Court evolved the principle of absolute liability for hazardous industries, linking environmental safety directly to the right to life.
- Subhash Kumar v. State of Bihar (1991): The Court explicitly held that the right to life includes the right to enjoy pollution-free water and air for full enjoyment of life.
- Virendra Gaur v. State of Haryana (1995): The Court emphasized that environmental protection is essential for the quality of life, thereby reinforcing environmental rights as part of Article 21.
- Vellore Citizens' Welfare Forum v. Union of India (1996): The SC recognized the precautionary principle and polluter pays principle as part of the law of the land, holding that

sustainable development is a constitutional mandate flowing from Article 21.

- A.P. Pollution Control Board v. Prof. M.V. Nayudu (1999): The Court highlighted the need for scientific expertise in environmental adjudication and reaffirmed the link between environmental protection and Article 21.

Constitutional Integration: The liberal interpretation of Article 21 has been reinforced by reading it harmoniously with Article 48A (Directive Principle to protect environment) and article 51A(g) (Fundamental Duty of citizens), thereby creating a holistic constitutional framework for environmental protection. This expansive interpretation has enabled Public Interest Litigation (PIL) in environmental matters, filled legislative gaps where statutory law was absent or weak, elevated environmental protection to the status of a fundamental right and strengthened judicial enforcement of sustainable development.

Through a liberal interpretation of Article 21, the Supreme Court has transformed environmental protection from a policy objective into a justiciable fundamental right, making it a powerful tool for safeguarding ecological balance, public health, and intergenerational equity in India. From the 1980s onward, PIL transformed the Supreme Court and High Courts into central environmental actors, interpreting the right to life under Article 21 to include a clean and healthy environment. Doctrines such as precautionary principle, polluter pays, and public trust were judicially imported and applied in cases on air pollution, forest diversions and industrial siting. The creation of National Green Tribunal (NGT) in 2010 institutionalized specialized adjudication for environmental disputes, improving access and formalizing technical review.

The National Environment Policy (NEP) 2006

The National Environment Policy 2006 marked a significant shift from earlier environmental strategies that were largely regulatory and command-and-control in nature. Policies prior to NEP 2006 focused heavily on pollution control through legislation such as the Water Act (1974), Air Act (1981), and the Environment Protection Act (1986). These laws emphasized compliance, standard-setting, and punitive action against violator, while it (NEP,2006) provided a comprehensive, umbrella framework linking forests, water, land, pollution, biodiversity, and climate issues under one policy vision. It marked a major step in India's approach to environmental governance by shifting from strict regulation-based control to a more integrated, participatory, and incentive-driven framework. It emphasized the principle of sustainable development, polluter pays, and public trust, aiming to balance economic growth with ecological protection. A key strength of the policy was its focus on mainstreaming environmental concerns across all sectors, including industry, agriculture, and infrastructure, and its recognition of local communities—especially forest dwellers and indigenous groups—as important environmental stewards. Increasingly, it emphasizes decentralization, community participation, and a mix of regulatory and market-based instruments. Contemporary priorities include climate action, biodiversity conservation, waste management, and resilience-building. Overall, India's environmental policy aims to balance ecological integrity with inclusive development.

The National Environment Policy (NEP) 2006, was a shift toward a more holistic and integrative framework for environmental governance. It attempted to consolidate earlier policies—such as the National Forest Policy (1988) and National Water Policy (2002)—into a unified vision grounded in sustainable development, equity, and the principles of the polluter pays and precautionary approach. NEP 2006 moved toward a policy-based and outcome-oriented framework. It emphasized balancing environmental protection with economic growth, recognizing that sustainable development should help, not hinder, livelihoods and poverty reduction. A key strength of the policy was its recognition that environmental protection must be mainstreamed across all sectors of the economy. Rather than treating the environment as an isolated domain, the policy acknowledged the interconnectedness of ecological health with poverty alleviation, agriculture, industry, and infrastructure. NEP 2006 also emphasized community participation, particularly the role of local and indigenous communities in resource management, which aligned with global trends in environmental governance. It led to introduction of a decentralized and participatory approach. Earlier policies treated environmental protection mainly as a responsibility of the Central and State Governments and regulatory agencies. In contrast, NEP 2006 highlighted the role of local communities, Panchayati Raj institutions, private sector stakeholders, and civil society. It stressed environmental stewardship and community-based conservation, especially in the management of forests, water resources, and biodiversity.

The NEP 2006 also broadened the environmental agenda beyond pollution abatement. Earlier frameworks focused on industrial and urban pollution, conservation of forests, and protection of wildlife through sector-specific programs. NEP 2006 broadened India's environmental agenda beyond pollution control to include ecosystem services, livelihoods, conservation, climate concerns, and environmental governance. NEP 2006 adopted a holistic "ecosystem-based management" approach, promoting the protection of fragile ecosystems such as the Himalayas, coasts, and wetlands, and introduced new themes like climate change adaptation, disaster management, and environmental governance reforms. It reflected India's increasing engagement with global environmental commitments and integrated international environmental agreements into national policy.

Earlier approach relied mostly on licensing, prohibitions, fines, and enforcement, the NEP 2006 introduced economic instruments like green taxes, tradable permits, and incentives for cleaner technology—tools that earlier approaches had barely emphasized. The policy recognized that market-based mechanisms can encourage compliance more effectively than strict legal enforcement alone. It also promoted public-private partnerships, valuing environmental services as economic assets and integrating the environment with sectors such as energy, infrastructure, and industry. Apart from these, it also introduced economic and market tools such as -polluter-pays principle, environmental taxes, tradable permits, incentives for clean technology and aimed to make environmental protection economically viable.

The NEP 2006 marked a major shift from the earlier fragmented and sector-specific environmental policies of the 1980s and 1990s. Earlier approaches—such as the National Forest Policy (1988), National Conservation Strategy (1992), and Policy Statement on Abatement of Pollution (1992)—were narrow in scope and dealt with issues in isolation. Modern challenges—urban pollution, industrial expansion, unsustainable agriculture—require cross-sector solutions. NEP 2006 stressed mainstreaming environmental concerns into energy, transport, industry, urban planning, agriculture, etc. This systems-based approach is even more important today as sectors interlink more strongly. NEP 2006 improved upon these by offering a comprehensive, integrated policy framework that linked environmental protection with economic and social development, recognizing that sustainability required a balance between conservation and livelihoods.

Earlier policies lacked a strong articulation of these principles, which limited effective prevention of environmental damage. NEP 2006 explicitly emphasized risk avoidance, cost internalization, and accountability of polluters, moving India closer to contemporary global environmental governance standards. Another significant enhancement was its strong focus on decentralized environmental management. Earlier policies were heavily top-down, often ignoring local realities. NEP 2006 recognized the crucial role of panchayats, urban local bodies, and community institutions, encouraging local-level planning, stakeholder participation, and community-based resource management. This shift aimed to empower people directly impacted by environmental decisions.

NEP 2006, also improved upon earlier approaches by adopting an ecosystem-based management strategy. Instead of addressing forests, water, air, and biodiversity separately, the policy advocated integrated management of ecosystems such as wetlands, coastal zones, mountains, and deserts. This represented a more scientific approach, acknowledging ecological interlinkages that earlier policies often overlooked. Unlike earlier policies focused mainly on conservation, NEP 2006 placed strong emphasis on environmental governance reforms, including improved transparency, improved environmental impact assessment (EIA) processes, better environmental information systems, use of economic instruments, and public–private partnerships. These governance reforms were largely absent in previous policies.

It emphasizes improved environmental information systems, and the use of technological tools signalled a modernized approach. India today faces data gaps in air quality, groundwater, biodiversity, and urban pollution. NEP 2006 called for better monitoring systems, public access to environmental data and use of technology for tracking degradation. This is directly relevant in an age of satellite monitoring, AI-based pollution tracking, and open-data platforms.

Finally, NEP 2006, strengthened the link between environment and human well-being, especially the poor. Earlier policies framed conservation largely in ecological terms; NEP 2006 recognized that environmental degradation disproportionately harms vulnerable groups. By aligning environmental protection with poverty reduction and sustainable livelihoods, the policy created a more inclusive and socially aware approach. India's rapid urbanization and infrastructure growth continue to strain ecosystems. The NEP's recommendations for strategic environmental assessment (SEA), sustainable urban planning, cleaner production technologies are highly applicable in managing modern megacities and industrial corridors.

However, the policy was often criticized for being broad and non-binding, with many recommendations lacking clear implementation mechanisms or legal force. It tended to rely heavily on market instruments, which some argued could dilute accountability. While it updated earlier environmental approaches and provided a coherent framework for future laws and programmes, its overall impact depended largely on how well its principles were translated into actionable regulations. Much of NEP 2006 consists of guiding principles rather than specific, enforceable mandates. NEP is a policy, not a law; it does not create enforceable obligations. Much relies on voluntary compliance and subordinate rules. It offers broad objectives without detailing measurable targets, timelines, or institutional responsibilities. This made it difficult for Central and State agencies to operationalize the policy, and it often remained aspirational rather than transformative. A major criticism is that NEP 2006 favored economic liberalization over environmental protection. The language of the policy strongly emphasizes "conservation with growth," which critics argue opened the door to greater flexibility for industries. For instance, its support for market-based instruments and public–private partnerships were welcomed by industry but raised concerns about prioritizing business interests over ecological safeguards, especially in fragile regions.

Another major criticism is the policy's heavy reliance on market-based instruments–such as tradable permits, fiscal incentives, and valuation of ecosystem services–to achieve environmental goals. While these tools can be effective, critics argue that in the Indian context, where regulatory capacity and enforcement remain weak, market instruments may enable polluters to avoid accountability. There are concerns that the policy implicitly favours economic growth and industrial expansion, sometimes at the cost of ecological integrity, by presenting environmental safeguards as negotiable rather than essential. Its push for economic instruments, public–private partnerships, and self-regulation invited criticism that it favours industry over strict regulatory control. Experts have also pointed out that NEP 2006 lacked integration with existing environmental laws, creating ambiguity. Instead of strengthening regulatory bodies like the Pollution Control Boards, the policy proposed parallel mechanisms such as accreditation agencies for environmental impact assessments. This risked undermining regulatory accountability and encouraged outsourcing of compliance to private entities.

Additionally, NEP 2006 has been critiqued for insufficiently addressing issues like climate change, urban pollution, and biodiversity loss with the urgency they require. Its treatment of environmental justice is also limited; although it acknowledges vulnerable communities, it does not establish strong mechanisms to protect them from disproportionate environmental harm. It does mention livelihoods of affected people, the policy insufficiently addresses displacement, inequality, and the rights of vulnerable communities affected by development projects. At that time, these issues were rapidly escalating, yet the policy provided only general statements instead of concrete roadmaps, leaving a critical gap in India's environmental strategy.

In conclusion, while the National Environment Policy 2006 was a progressive attempt to modernize India's environmental governance, its practical impact has been constrained by vague commitments, inadequate enforcement strategies, and over-dependence on market solutions. To be truly effective, environmental policy must be grounded in actionable mandates, stronger regulatory frameworks, and a clearer balance between economic development and ecological preservation. While conceptually rich, the policy lacked time-bound targets, funding mechanisms, or a monitoring framework.

The National Green Tribunal (NGT) Act, 2010

The National Green Tribunal (NGT) Act, 2010, was enacted to establish a dedicated judicial body for expeditious and specialized adjudication of environmental disputes. India became one of the few countries to set up a separate environmental court system, reflecting the growing need for effective enforcement of environmental rights and obligations. The Act operationalized the constitutional guarantee under Article 21, which includes the right to a clean and healthy environment. National Green Tribunal (NGT) is constituted under the NGT Act, 2010 as a specialized environmental court to adjudicate civil cases related to environmental protection, conservation of forests, and natural resources. The Tribunal is designed as a multi-member, expert body, combining judicial and scientific expertise to ensure informed decision-making in technical environmental matters.

The Act created the National Green Tribunal, a quasi-judicial body, with expertise in environmental law, science, and technical matters. It provides the NGT with jurisdiction over all civil cases relating to the environment that arise under seven major laws, including the Environment (Protection) Act, 1986; Water Act, 1974; Air Act, 1981; Forest Conservation Act, 1980; and Public Liability Insurance Act, 1991. This integration ensures that disputes across multiple environmental legislations can be handled in one specialized forum. A key feature of the Act is its emphasis on speedy justice. The NGT is mandated to dispose of cases within six months, significantly reducing delays associated with traditional courts. It applies principles such as polluter pays, precautionary principle, and sustainable development while delivering its judgments, giving these environmental doctrines strong legal standing in India. The Tribunal's powers include awarding relief and compensation, ordering restoration of damaged ecosystems, and issuing directions to halt or regulate harmful activities.

The Act also lays down a structured system of benches, including a Principal Bench in New Delhi and zonal benches across India, making environmental justice accessible. It allows appeals to the Supreme Court but restricts the High Courts' jurisdiction over matters within the NGT's domain, helping maintain uniformity in environmental rulings. Overall, the National Green Tribunal Act, 2010 represents a major institutional reform in India's environmental governance. By combining judicial authority with technical expertise and ensuring time-bound resolution, it strengthens environmental rule of law and provides citizens with an effective mechanism to challenge ecological degradation.

The NGT consists of a Chairperson, Judicial Members, and Expert Members. The Chairperson must be a retired Supreme Court Judge or a Chief Justice of a High Court. Judicial Members are required to be sitting or retired High Court judges. Expert Members are appointed from fields such as environmental science, ecology, forestry, climate studies, pollution control, or related disciplines, ensuring that technical aspects of environmental disputes are understood and evaluated effectively.

Appointments are made by the Central Government, but the selection process includes consultation with the Chief Justice of India for the Chairperson, ensuring independence and judicial oversight. Members serve a fixed tenure (typically 5 years) and must retire at specified age limits (70 years for Chairperson and Judicial Members; 67 years for Expert Members). The Tribunal operates through its Principal Bench in New Delhi and four Zonal Benches (Bhopal, Pune, Kolkata, and Chennai), each with circuit benches to improve accessibility. The Act emphasizes a balanced composition: each bench must include at least one Judicial Member and one Expert Member, enabling a blended approach to environmental adjudication. Overall, the constitution of the NGT ensures independence, expertise, and regional accessibility, making it a uniquely structured body for effective environmental governance in India.

Major landmark judgments by the National Green Tribunal since 2010

The National Green Tribunal (NGT), established in 2011, has delivered several landmark judgments advancing environmental protection through principles like polluter pays and sustainable development.

Waste Management

Almitra H. Patel vs. Union of India (2016): Mandated implementation of Solid Waste Management Rules 2016 across States/UTs, absolute segregation at waste-to-energy plants, buffer zones around landfills, and complete ban on open burning of waste, addressing daily generation of over 133,000 MT of untreated garbage.

Biodiversity and Forests

Save Mon Region Federation vs. Union of India (2013): Suspended environmental clearance for a ₹6,400 crore hydro project in Arunachal Pradesh to protect the black-necked crane (Schedule I species) and habitats of snow leopards, red pandas.

Rat-hole Coal Mining Ban, Meghalaya (2014): Banned unscientific rat-hole mining due to environmental degradation and safety risks.

POSCO Steel Plant, Odisha (2012): Suspended clearance for a 12 MT steel project, prioritizing tribal forest rights and ecology.

Pollution Control

Art of Living vs. Yamuna Floodplains (2016): Imposed ₹5 crore fine on the event organizer for damaging Yamuna floodplains, ordering restoration.

Ganga Pollution (2017): Directed comprehensive clean up, banning waste/effluent disposal and mandating sewage treatment plants.

MV Rak Ship Sinking (2016): Applied polluter pays, ordering ₹100 crore compensation from shipping entities for oil spill damaging mangroves/marine life.

Air Quality & Others

- Diwali Firecrackers Ban (2020): Temporarily prohibited sale/use of firecrackers in Delhi-NCR to curb festival-related pollution spikes.
- Diesel Vehicles Ban (2015): Barred >10-year-old diesel vehicles in Delhi-NCR; regulated new registrations to reduce emissions.
- NGT v. NHAI Construction Dust (2023): Levied ₹2 crore penalty under polluter pays for dust pollution from highway projects.

India's environmental policies since 2010

India's environmental policies since 2010 emphasize renewable energy expansion, forest restoration, and regulatory reforms under the National Action Plan on Climate Change (NAPCC) missions, strengthening of sectoral rules: Plastic Waste Management (2016), Solid Waste Management (2016), E-Waste (Management) Rules (2016) and their later amendments (including EPR expansions through 2022–2024). The 2016 suite (plastic, e-waste, solid waste management) moved India from vague targets to enforceable producer obligations (EPR), duties on municipalities and standards for recyclers. This created legal levers to hold producers and local bodies accountable. Frequent amendments (e.g., e-waste rules updated through 2023–24) show regulators responding to new technologies and compliance gaps rather than leaving rules unchanged. However, EPR has shifted responsibility to producers, but effective EPR needs: traceable producer registries, credible recycler networks, auditing and sanctions.

Another important National programme launched by MoEFCC had been National Clean Air Programme (NCAP) in 2019. It aims to tackle the growing problem of air pollution in a comprehensive and time-bound manner. It is a long-term, national-level strategy aimed at improving air quality across the country through coordinated action between Central, State, and Local governments. The primary objective of NCAP is to achieve a 20%–30% reduction in $PM_{2.5}$ and PM_{10} concentrations by 2024, using 2017 as the base year (later targets have been made more ambitious in subsequent revisions). The programme initially covered 102 non-attainment cities—cities that consistently failed to meet National Ambient Air Quality Standards (NAAQS)—and later expanded to 130+ cities. NCAP adopts a multi-sectoral and collaborative approach. It focuses on key pollution sources such as vehicular emissions, industrial pollution, construction dust, road dust, waste burning, and household fuel use. Major components include: city-specific action plans prepared by State governments, strengthening air quality monitoring networks, promotion of cleaner technologies and fuels, public awareness and citizen participation and capacity building of pollution control boards. The programme emphasizes cooperative federalism, with funding support through the 15th Finance Commission grants and convergence with schemes like AMRUT, Smart Cities Mission, Swachh Bharat Mission, and FAME (electric mobility). NCAP is not a standalone law but a policy framework under the Ministry of Environment, Forest and Climate Change (MoEFCC). It represents a shift from reactive to preventive and data-driven air quality management. However, challenges remain in enforcement, inter-agency coordination, and sustained local capacity. Despite limitations, NCAP marks a significant step toward institutionalizing air quality governance in India.

India's environmental policy since independence has evolved from a resource-extraction focus inherited from colonial times to a comprehensive framework post- 1972 Stockholm Conference, marked by key legislations like the Wildlife Protection Act (1972), Water Act (1974), Forest Conservation Act (1980), and Environment Protection Act (1986), driven by crises such as Bhopal and judicial activism. Constitutional mandates via the 42nd Amendment (Articles 48A and 51A(g)) elevated environmental protection as a State directive and citizen duty. Judicial interventions expanded Article 21 to include the right to a clean environment, enforcing polluter pays and sustainable development principles through landmark cases. From the 1980s onward, Public Interest Litigation (PIL) transformed the Supreme Court and High Courts into central environmental actors, interpreting the right to life under Article 21 to include a clean and healthy environment. Doctrines such as precautionary principle, polluter pays, and public trust were judicially imported and applied in cases on air pollution, forest diversions and industrial siting. The National Environment Policy 2006 marked a major step in India's approach to environmental governance by shifting from strict regulation-based control to a more integrated, participatory, and incentive-driven framework. It emphasized the principle of sustainable development, polluter pays, and public trust, aiming to balance economic growth with ecological protection. A key strength of the policy was its focus on mainstreaming environmental concerns across all sectors, including industry, agriculture, and infrastructure, and its recognition of local communities—especially forest dwellers and indigenous groups—as important environmental stewards. India's approach links environmental protection with economic development through environment impact assessment, sustainable resource use, and land-use planning. Increasingly, it emphasizes decentralization, community participation, and a mix of regulatory and market-based instruments. Contemporary priorities include climate action, biodiversity conservation, waste management, and resilience-building. The creation of NGT in 2010 institutionalized specialized adjudication for environmental disputes, improving access and formalizing technical review. Overall, India's environmental policy aims to balance ecological integrity with inclusive development. An attempt has been made to categorize evolution of environmental policy in terms of different phases and highlight major developments during that period to get better insight and it is given at following table:

Phase	Time period	Key Drivers	Major Developments	Outcomes/Challenges
Colonial/ Post-Colonial	Pre-1947 to 1971	Revenue extraction, development needs (e.g., railways)	Indian Forest Act 1927; minimal shift post-independence.	Resource exploitation prioritized over conservation; no holistic policy.
Post-Stockholm Awakening	1972-1984	UN Stockholm Conference; PM Indira Gandhi's participation	Wildlife Protection Act 1972; Water Act 1974; Air Act 1981; 42nd Amendment (Articles 48A, 51A(g)); National Council for Environmental Planning.	Established pollution boards, constitutional mandates; reactive to global cues but limited enforcement.
Crisis Response, Umbrella Laws & Judicial Era	1985-1990s	Bhopal disaster 1984; Delhi gas leak and Public Interest Litigation	Environment Protection Act 1986; Forest Conservation Act 1980; M/o Environment and Forest formation in 1985, EIA notification 1994.	Centralized powers, sectoral laws; addressed pollution but implementation gaps emerged. Doctrines like precautionary principle, polluter pays, public trust, etc. were applied.
Sustainable Era	2000s-Present	Climate commitments ,liberalization	National Environment Policy 2006, FRA 2006, NAPCC 2008, NGT 2010.	Persistent enforcement issues.

Overall, implementation of environmental policy remains weak due to bureaucratic inefficiencies, corruption, inadequate enforcement by bodies like CPCB/SPCBs, and centralized powers fostering arbitrariness without sufficient State or public involvement. Policies often react to crises rather than proactively balancing economic growth with ecology, leading to persistent issues like pollution, deforestation, and EIA loopholes amid rapid industrialization. Resource constraints and poor inter-agency coordination exacerbate gaps, rendering many laws symbolic. While policy proliferation post-1972 signifies progress, the over reliance on judiciary over executive action highlights governance failures, with economic liberalization prioritizing growth over sustainability. Recent reforms like NGT (2010) offer promise but falter on ground-level execution, underscoring needs for decentralized enforcement, community participation, and capacity building.

Influence of International Conferences and Summit on Indian Environmental Policy

India's environmental policy has evolved significantly since the 1970s, shaped not only by domestic ecological pressures but also by global environmental diplomacy. International agreements, conventions, and multilateral summit and conferences have played a decisive role in transforming India's legislative frameworks, policy instruments, institutional mechanisms, and governance approach. From early engagement in the Stockholm Conference (1972) to the contemporary climate negotiations under the UNFCCC, these global events have catalyzed both normative and regulatory shifts. The influence has been visible in the framing of foundational laws, creation of institutions, adoption of global best practices, and alignment of national strategies with international environmental commitments.

One of the earliest influences came from The Club of Rome, founded in 1968, significantly shaped global thinking on environment-development linkages through its landmark 1972 report "The Limits to Growth." Although not directly involved in India's policy-making, its ideas profoundly influenced India's environmental discourse, planning philosophy, and regulatory evolution from the 1970s onward. Its 1972 report "The Limits to Growth" highlighted the dangers of unchecked population growth, pollution and resource exhaustion, creating an intellectual shift that resonated with Indian planners. Its emphasis on long-term sustainability, scientific planning and sustainable development. These ideas echoed strongly in India's Fourth and Fifth Five-Year Plans, which began integrating environmental concerns for the first time. The National Committee on Environmental Planning and Coordination (NCEPC) (1972), India's first national environmental body, was created in the same year—reflecting a shift toward structured environmental oversight in line with global sustainability debates triggered by the Club of Rome. Though, The Club of Rome did not directly influenced India's environmental policy, but it played a decisive intellectual and philosophical role by shaping global thinking about sustainable growth, ecological limits, and systemic environmental risks. India's shift toward structured environmental governance, sustainability-oriented planning, and long-term resource management reflects the diffusion of these global ideas into national policy frameworks.

The earliest direct and perceptible major influence came from the 1972 United Nations Conference on the Human Environment (Stockholm Conference). India's participation in this landmark summit encouraged the recognition of environmental protection as a national priority. As a direct outcome, environmental provisions were incorporated into the Indian Constitution through the 42nd Amendment, adding Article 48A (Directive Principles) and Article 51A(g) (Fundamental Duties) which mandate the protection of environment and biodiversity. This summit also laid the intellectual groundwork for subsequent environmental legislation in the 1980s and beyond.

Another significant influence emerged from the 1992 Rio Earth Summit (United Nations Conference on Environment and Development, UNCED). This Summit led to global agreements such as the Convention on Biological Diversity (CBD), the United Nations Framework Convention on Climate Change (UNFCCC), and Agenda 21. India became a signatory to all three, which resulted in major domestic actions. The CBD inspired the Biological Diversity Act (2002) and the creation of bodies like the National Biodiversity Authority. Agenda 21 encouraged sustainable development planning, community participation and environmental education across States. Rio's Declaration on Environment and Development explicitly urged countries to use "economic instruments" and to internalize environmental costs, framed through Principle 16 (polluter pays principle). This principle states that national authorities should promote internalization of environmental costs and use economic instruments so that polluters bear the cost of pollution, subject to public interest and trade considerations. This moved environmental policy discourse beyond pure command-and-control regulation and legitimized/popularized Market Based Instruments (MBI) such as taxes, charges, and tradable permits at the international level.

Agenda 21, the Summit's main action plan, repeatedly links sustainable development to better management of natural resources using open and efficient markets, trade policies, and pricing reforms. Its "Means of Implementation" sections encourage countries to reform subsidies, use environmental charges, and integrate environment into fiscal and trade policy, which directly underpins later adoption of environmental taxes, user charges, and incentive schemes. By framing these as tools for "sustainable development" rather than just pollution control, Agenda 21 broadened the scope of MBI to energy, agriculture, water, and waste.

International environmental agreements have also shaped India's sector-specific policies. The Montreal Protocol led to the Ozone Depleting Substances Rules and a phased reduction of chemicals harmful to the ozone layer. The Basel, Rotterdam, and Stockholm Conventions influenced India's waste management rules, chemical safety norms, and hazardous substance regulations. Similarly, global conventions on wildlife, such as Convention on International Trade in Endangered Species of Wild Fauna and Flora (CITES), strengthened India's wildlife conservation laws and enforcement mechanisms.

Perhaps the most influential set of conferences for India has been the UNFCCC Conference of Parties (CoP) meetings. The Kyoto Protocol (1997) shaped India's early climate policies, enabling the growth of renewable energy and energy-efficiency projects through Clean Development Mechanism (CDM) funding. The Paris Conference of Parties (COP-21), held in December 2015 under the UNFCCC, marked a historic milestone in global climate governance with the adoption of the Paris Agreement. Its central objective is to limit the rise in global average temperature to well below 2°C above pre-industrial levels, while pursuing efforts to limit warming to 1.5°C. The Agreement introduced Nationally Determined Contributions (NDCs), allowing countries to set their own mitigation and adaptation targets based on national circumstances, with a mechanism for periodic review and enhanced ambition every five years. It emphasized climate finance, committing developed countries to mobilize USD 100 billion annually to support developing nations. The Agreement also strengthened focus on adaptation, loss and damage, transparency, and technology transfer. For developing countries like India, the Paris Agreement balanced climate responsibility with the principles of equity and common but differentiated responsibilities, making it a flexible yet universal climate framework. Later, the Paris Agreement (2015) had a transformative impact, requiring India to submit its Nationally

Determined Contributions (NDCs). This triggered ambitious national targets such as reducing the emission intensity of GDP, expanding forest cover, and accelerating renewable energy deployment. Subsequent summits, such as COP26 in Glasgow, strengthened India's policy commitments through the "Panchamrit" pledges, which include increasing non-fossil energy capacity and achieving net-zero emissions by 2070.

The key time phases can be summarized in a given table:

Phase	Key Conference	Policy Impacts
Pre-1972	None major	Limited; domestic focus
1972-1984	Stockholm 1972	Foundational laws, constitutional duties, establishment of Ministry of Environment and Forest
1985-1990s	Montreal 1987, Rio 1992	Umbrella Acts, EIA, sustainability
2000s-Present	Kyoto 1997, Paris 2015, CBD	NAPCC, NGT, NDCs, global compliance

India achieved the 50% non-fossil fuel power capacity target in June 2025, five years ahead of the 2030 deadline, with installed solar capacity rising over 41 times to 116.25 GW by mid-2025. Emission intensity of GDP dropped 36% between 2005 and 2020, placing India on track to meet or exceed its Nationally Determined Contributions (NDC) goals despite low per capita emissions. At CoP30 in November 2025, Environment Minister, Shri Bhupender Yadav announced India will submit revised NDCs for 2035 by December, 2025 alongside its first Biennial Transparency Report, emphasizing implementation and calling for developed nations' finance commitments. These updates align with India's net-zero goal by 2070 and Panchamrit pledges from COP26.

India's environmental policy has not developed in isolation. It has drawn heavily from global environmental discourses–ranging from the 1972 Stockholm Conference and the Rio Earth Summit to the SDGs and the Paris Agreement. These global commitments nudged India toward sustainable development pathways, culminating in visionary national frameworks such as the National Environment Policy (2006) and the National Action Plan on Climate Change (2008). These documents marked an evolution from command-and-control regulation to a more holistic model that incorporates economic instruments, community participation, environmental valuation, and mission-mode interventions. Summit conferences promote cooperation, climate finance, and technology transfer, enabling India to implement large-scale renewable energy projects, improve disaster management, and invest in climate adaptation. Platforms such as the International Solar Alliance (launched after the Paris Agreement) demonstrate how India is not only influenced by global agreements but also emerging as a leader in shaping them.

International agreements and global summit conferences have exerted profound influence on the evolution of India's environmental policy. They have not only shaped India's legislative and regulatory frameworks but also reoriented national priorities towards sustainable development, biodiversity conservation, climate resilience, and global environmental leadership. The trajectory from Stockholm to Paris, and onward to emerging biodiversity and climate commitments, reveals a progressive deepening of India's environmental governance. While domestic challenges remain substantial–pollution, climate vulnerability, biodiversity loss–the influence of global environmental diplomacy continues to push India toward more robust, science-based, integrated environmental policies. In the decades ahead, India's engagement in multilateral environmental processes will remain central to balancing development imperatives with ecological stewardship.

Chapter 2:

Environmental Governance Architecture: Institutions Shaping Environment Policies in India

Role of the Ministry of Environment, Forest and Climate Change (MoEFCC) in India's Environmental Policy

The Ministry of Environment, Forest and Climate Change (MoEFCC) is the apex institution responsible for shaping, implementing, and monitoring India's environmental policy. As the central environmental authority, it frames laws, sets national standards, coordinates with States, regulates natural resource use, enforces pollution controls, protects biodiversity, and steers India's climate action framework. The MoEFCC Annual Report, 2023-24 provides a comprehensive account of activities across the Ministry's mandate – environment, forests, wildlife, pollution control, biodiversity, wetlands/coastal zones, climate change, policy & regulation, environmental clearances, and public awareness/education. It also outlines the Ministry's role under India's national laws and international environmental commitments, including climate conventions, biodiversity treaties and conventions on hazardous substances.

MoEFCC's most visible role is formulating environmental legislation and rules. It administers cornerstone laws such as the Environment (Protection) Act 1986, Air Act 1981, Water Act 1974, Wildlife Protection Act 1972, and Forest Conservation Act 1980. Through these laws, the Ministry establishes standards for emissions, effluents, waste management, and environmental clearance processes. The ministry continuously updates rules for pollution control, hazardous waste, plastics, e-waste, biomedical waste, and coastal zone regulation, ensuring regulatory alignment with emerging environmental challenges.

A core responsibility of MoEFCC is the Environmental Impact Assessment (EIA) process. The Ministry issues Environmental Clearance (EC) and Coastal Regulation Zone (CRZ) clearance for major infrastructure and industrial projects, ensuring that environmental safeguards, mitigation plans, and compliance conditions are built into project lifecycles. Through the EIA Notification (1994, 2006, and amendments), the Ministry integrates environmental considerations into national economic planning.

MoEFCC also plays a crucial role in pollution control and environmental monitoring. It supervises the Central Pollution Control Board (CPCB), which sets national ambient air and water quality standards, coordinates State pollution control boards, and enforces compliance. In natural resource management, MoEFCC is the nodal agency for forest governance, wildlife conservation, and biodiversity protection. It regulates diversion of forest land for non-forest purposes, manages protected areas, and implements key national missions such as the Green India Mission and Project Tiger. The National Biodiversity Authority and State Biodiversity Boards also function under its supervision, ensuring conservation, sustainable use, and equitable sharing of biological resources.

MoEFCC is at the forefront of India's climate change policy. It formulates climate strategies, updates India's Nationally Determined Contributions (NDCs), and coordinates national missions under the National Action Plan on Climate Change (NAPCC). It represents India in international climate negotiations (UNFCCC, CBD, Montreal Protocol), manages national GHG inventories, spearheads adaptation and mitigation programmes, and guides inter-ministerial climate coordination.

Another important role is environmental governance and decentralization. Through policies such as the National Environment Policy (NEP) 2006, the ministry promotes principles of sustainable development, public participation, environmental transparency, and environmental justice. Institutions like the National Green Tribunal (NGT) and CAMPA operate within MoEFCC's policy framework.

MoEFCC also invests in research, education, and awareness, supporting environmental research institutions, pollution monitoring networks, the ENVIS system, and mass awareness campaigns. It provides funding for State-level environmental programmes, capacity building for pollution regulators, and implementation support for green technologies.

In summary, MoEFCC acts as the central architect of India's environmental policy, balancing conservation and development through law-making, regulation, monitoring, climate action, natural resource stewardship, and international environmental diplomacy. Its role is foundational to India's pursuit of sustainable development and ecological security.

The Ministry of Environment, Forest and Climate Change (MoEFCC) implements several flagship schemes that form the backbone of India's environmental policy. These schemes address diverse issues such as pollution control, forest conservation, biodiversity protection, climate change mitigation, and environmental awareness. Collectively, they operationalize the constitutional mandate of environmental protection under Articles 48A and 51A(g) and support India's commitments under global environmental agreements.

Green India Mission (GIM) is one of the eight key missions under India's National Action Plan on Climate Change (NAPCC), launched in 2010. Implemented by the Ministry of Environment, Forest and Climate Change (MoEFCC), the mission seeks to enhance India's forest and tree cover as a core climate adaptation and mitigation strategy. Its fundamental objective is to restore degraded ecosystems, increase carbon sequestration, improve biodiversity, and secure the livelihoods of forest-dependent communities. GIM marks a shift in India's forest sector policy—from a pure conservation approach to a climate-resilient, people-centric, and landscape-based strategy. It also contributes to India's Nationally Determined Contributions (NDCs) by enhancing carbon sinks.

At its core, GIM aims to increase forest/tree cover on 5 million hectares of land and improve the quality of forest cover on an additional 5 million hectares. This involves afforestation, reforestation, ecological restoration, and sustainable management of natural ecosystems such as forests, grasslands, wetlands, and agroforestry landscapes. The mission adopts a landscape-level approach, recognizing that ecosystems function across administrative boundaries and require integrated restoration strategies.

One of the most significant contributions of the mission is its focus on climate resilience. By strengthening ecosystem services—soil stability, hydrological cycles, and carbon storage—GIM enhances India's capacity to cope with climate-induced stresses like floods, droughts, and extreme temperatures. Forests are treated not merely as carbon sinks but as multi-functional systems supporting biodiversity, water security, and community livelihoods.

GIM also emphasizes a participatory, community-based governance model. It integrates local institutions such as Joint Forest Management Committees (JFMCs), Gram Sabhas, Van Panchayats, and Self-Help Groups into planning and implementation. This approach reinforces democratic forest governance and ensures that afforestation activities are aligned with the needs of local communities—especially tribal groups who depend on forests for fuelwood, fodder, medicinal plants, and non-timber forest products (NTFPs). The mission promotes livelihood diversification through eco-tourism, NTFP value chains, and sustainable agriculture practices.

The mission's design incorporates convergence across ministries, including Rural Development, Agriculture, Tribal Affairs, Water Resources, and Urban Development. This integration is significant because landscape restoration requires coordination in watershed management, soil conservation, community development, and rural employment through schemes such as MGNREGA. Convergence helps in mobilizing financial resources and ensures that GIM activities are embedded in broader rural development programmes.

A central element of GIM is its reliance on scientific planning, including baseline studies, vulnerability assessments, species suitability mapping, and monitoring through remote sensing and GIS (geographic information system). The mission encourages the use of indigenous species, mixed plantations, and biodiversity-rich restoration instead of monoculture plantations, aligning with ecological principles.

Despite its ambitious goals, GIM has faced challenges. Funding gaps, slow disbursement, limited capacity in local institutions, and variable implementation across States have constrained its full potential. It also overlaps with CAMPA-funded afforestation, and occasional prioritization of plantations over natural regeneration, have also been concerns. Nonetheless, recent policy efforts–including strengthened monitoring, increased budgetary support, and alignment with carbon markets–are revitalizing the mission.

Another key initiative is **Compensatory Afforestation Fund Management and Planning Authority (CAMPA) scheme**. CAMPA manages funds collected when forest lands are diverted for non-forest activities. These funds are utilized by States for afforestation, regeneration of degraded forests, and strengthening of forest protection. CAMPA ensures that ecological losses are compensated through systematic planning, thereby integrating environmental safeguards into infrastructure and industrial development. Though adhoc CAMPA existed since 2006, the system was institutionalized through the Compensatory Afforestation Fund Act, 2016, and became operational in 2018. Administered by the Ministry of Environment, Forest and Climate Change (MoEFCC), CAMPA ensures that the ecological loss due to forest diversion is scientifically compensated through afforestation and ecosystem restoration. Under the scheme, project developers who divert forest land must pay for Compensatory Afforestation (CA), Net Present Value (NPV) of forests, and costs for catchment management, wildlife conservation, and forest protection measures. These funds are deposited in the National Compensatory Afforestation Fund (managed by National CAMPA) and transferred to State CAMPA authorities, who implement on-ground activities.

Funds under CAMPA are used for a wide range of interventions—raising new plantations, assisted natural regeneration, soil and moisture conservation works, forest fire prevention, wildlife habitat improvement, strengthening forest protection infrastructure, and community-based conservation initiatives. The Act provides a legally robust framework to ensure transparency, accountability, and timely utilization of the large pool of funds (accumulated to more than ₹50,000 crore at the time of operationalization).

A key strength of CAMPA is that it mainstreams the "polluter pays" principle, ensuring that entities diverting forests internalize ecological costs. It also enables long-term financing for India's forest management strategy, complementing programmes like the Green India Mission. A major criticism of CAMPA is its over-reliance on plantation-based afforestation, often prioritizing monoculture species such as eucalyptus or teak. Such plantations provide limited biodiversity value, offer poor ecosystem services, and may negatively impact groundwater. This departs from the ecological principles of restoring natural forest ecosystems. Another concern is the poor quality and survival rate of plantations. Several audits by the CAG and independent researchers have highlighted gaps between funds released, land availability, and actual afforestation outcomes. In many States, land identified for compensatory afforestation is degraded, encroached, or ecologically unsuitable, undermining the objective of replacing lost forest cover.

Eco-Label Scheme, popularly known as Ecomark, is a flagship environmental labeling programme launched by the Ministry of Environment, Forest and Climate Change (MoEFCC) in 1991. Its primary purpose is to identify and certify products that have a reduced environmental impact throughout their life cycle—production, use, and disposal. The scheme embodies India's commitment to sustainable consumption, circular economy principles, and green market transformation. Ecomark is awarded to consumer products that meet both quality and environmental criteria, ensuring that environmentally superior products are also safe, durable and reliable. Bureau of Indian Standards (BIS) acts as the implementing agency responsible for assessment, certification, and granting the label, while MoEFCC formulates the environmental criteria for each product category. This dual institutional mechanism strengthens the credibility, scientific soundness, and market acceptance of the scheme.

The importance of the Eco-Label Scheme lies in its ability to use market-based incentives for environmental protection. By signalling eco-friendly products through a trusted label, it encourages manufacturers to adopt greener production technologies, reduce emissions, minimize waste, optimize resource efficiency, and use recyclable or biodegradable materials. For consumers, Ecomark acts as an information tool, enabling them to choose products that are safer and more environmentally responsible. In a market where environmental claims are often unverified, the Ecomark provides third-party assurance, reducing information asymmetry and promoting informed, sustainable consumer behavior. The scheme covers a wide range of product categories such as soaps and detergents, paints, paper, plastic bags, food items, packaging materials, textiles, and batteries. For each category, MoEFCC develops product-specific environmental criteria, typically focusing on parameters such as reduction in toxic substances, pollution control during manufacturing, energy efficiency, biodegradability, recyclability, and minimal resource extraction. These criteria are periodically updated to incorporate new technology, global standards, and India's evolving environmental priorities.

Beyond environmental benefits, Ecomark strengthens India's transition toward a green economy. It supports industrial competitiveness by encouraging industries to adopt modern clean technologies and meet global sustainability benchmarks. In international markets, where eco-labels influence consumer choice and regulatory acceptance, Ecomark-certified products gain a competitive edge. It also aligns with India's commitments under the Sustainable Development Goals (SDGs), particularly SDG 12 (responsible consumption and production).

The Eco-Label Scheme also contributes to reducing environmental externalities and the overall ecological footprint of consumer goods. By encouraging life-cycle thinking, it shifts attention from end-of-pipe pollution control to proactive environmental management. This helps in reducing solid waste generation, limiting hazardous chemicals, and promoting circular material flows.

Despite its potential, the Ecomark Scheme faces challenges including low consumer awareness, limited industry participation, and slow criteria development for new product categories. Weak marketing, absence of mandatory requirements, and competition from more widely recognized international eco-labels have limited its impact. However, recent government efforts to revive the scheme—such as expanding product coverage, aligning with global eco-standards, and integrating it with procurement policies—are improving its relevance.

National Clean Air Programme (NCAP), launched in January 2019 by India's Ministry of Environment, Forest and Climate Change (MoEFCC), targets a 40% reduction in particulate matter (PM10 and PM2.5) concentrations by 2026 in 132 non-attainment cities, using 2017 as the base year. NCAP adopts a collaborative, multi-sectoral approach, integrating central schemes like the 15th Finance Commission grants for air quality improvement. NCAP seeks to strengthen ambient air quality monitoring networks, foster public outreach for data dissemination, and develop city-specific action plans for pollution abatement. Key goals include augmenting monitoring stations, capacity building for state pollution control boards, and ensuring inclusive stakeholder participation from Central Ministries, States/UTs, and Local Bodies. The programme mainstreams existing policies like the National Action Plan on Climate Change, emphasizing convergence across sectors for preventive measures.

Action plans address multiple pollution sources: stubble burning prevention, industrial emission controls, vehicular pollution mitigation via cleaner fuels and public transport, dust suppression from construction and roads, and power generator regulations. Cities receive tailored annual reduction targets (3%-15% for PM10), with performance-linked funding; 82 cities aim for 40% overall cuts, while 49 under Fifteenth Finance Commission grants target 15% yearly. Tools like real-time monitoring via PRANA portal and green infrastructure promotion support implementation.

The Central Pollution Control Board (CPCB) coordinates NCAP, with city-level committees overseeing plans and inter-ministerial groups involving NITI Aayog and health ministries. Progress includes enhanced monitoring (over 4,000 stations), but challenges persist. Recent assessments urge reforms for stricter timelines and source apportionment studies. Under the National Clean Air Programme (NCAP), MoEFCC latest reports measurable improvements in 131 non-attainment cities are being monitored, and many have shown reductions in PM10 pollution compared with earlier years. NCAP positions India towards SDG11 (sustainable cities) and aligns with global commitments, complementing water-focused schemes like Namami Gange and DDWS efforts by addressing air-water pollution synergies, such as agricultural runoff and urban effluents.

The MoEFCC also implements **National Coastal Zone Management Programme (NCZMP)** is a major initiative of the Ministry of Environment, Forest and Climate Change (MoEFCC) aimed at protecting India's long and ecologically sensitive coastline. The programme operationalizes the objectives of the Coastal Regulation Zone (CRZ) Notifications, promotes sustainable development of coastal areas, and strengthens the resilience of coastal communities to climate change impacts such as cyclones, erosion, sea-level rise, and saline intrusion. NCZMP is implemented with support from the World Bank and State coastal zone management authorities, reflecting a collaborative, multi-level governance model.

India has a coastline of over 7,500 km, supporting rich biodiversity—mangroves, coral reefs, estuaries, lagoons, wetlands—and millions of people dependent on coastal ecosystems for fisheries, tourism, and livelihoods. However, rapid urbanization, industrialization, ports, erosion, waste disposal, and climate-driven hazards have severely stressed these ecosystems. NCZMP addresses these challenges through a combination of conservation, planning, restoration, and regulatory enforcement.

A central objective of NCZMP is the preparation and implementation of Integrated Coastal Zone Management Plans (ICZMPs) for each coastal State and union territory. These plans map ecological zones, hazard lines, shoreline changes, and permissible land-use activities, thereby guiding infrastructure development while ensuring environmental protection. The programme strengthens scientific capacity through high-resolution coastal mapping, creation of a National Centre for Sustainable Coastal Management (NCSCM) in Chennai, and development of coastal vulnerability indices.

NCZMP promotes eco-restoration of degraded coastal ecosystems. Key activities include mangrove plantation and regeneration, coral reef restoration, dune stabilization, wetland rejuvenation, and conservation of critical habitats for marine species such as sea turtles. These actions not only enhance biodiversity but also serve as natural buffers against storm surges and cyclones, embodying nature-based climate adaptation.

The programme also invests in coastal infrastructure resilience. This includes building multipurpose cyclone shelters, strengthening embankments, installing early warning systems, improving evacuation routes, and enhancing disaster preparedness capacities of coastal communities. By integrating climate resilience into coastal development, NCZMP contributes directly to the Sendai Framework for Disaster Risk Reduction and India's National Adaptation goals.

Equally important is the programme's emphasis on livelihood support and community participation. NCZMP works with fisher folk, coastal panchayats, women's self-help groups, and local enterprises to promote sustainable fishing, eco-friendly tourism, organic aquaculture, and skill development. By reducing dependence on ecologically sensitive zones and creating alternative income opportunities, NCZMP builds social resilience and ensures community ownership of conservation measures.

Regulatory strengthening is another pillar of NCZMP. The programme enhances the capacity of State Coastal Zone Management Authorities (SCZMAs) for CRZ enforcement, monitoring of coastal projects, and environmental clearance processes. Digital platforms, GIS tools, and real-time monitoring systems help identify violations and manage coastal resources more transparently.

Overall, the National Coastal Zone Management Programme represents India's integrated approach to balancing ecological sustainability with economic development along its vulnerable coastline. By combining scientific planning, ecosystem restoration, infrastructure resilience, and community-based governance, NCZMP plays a pivotal role in safeguarding coastal ecosystems and reducing climate-related risks.

Biodiversity conservation is strengthened through schemes like Project Tiger, Project Elephant, and Project Snow Leopard. Together, they safeguard India's ecological heritage, strengthen wildlife governance, and promote landscape-level conservation. These schemes safeguard India's rich wildlife heritage and natural ecosystems.

Project Tiger is India's oldest and most successful species-conservation programme. Initiated in 1973, it aims to ensure a viable population of wild tigers, restore their habitats, and reduce the ecological pressures on tiger landscapes. The programme is administered through the National Tiger Conservation Authority (NTCA). Its core strategy includes creating Tiger Reserves, where habitat protection, scientific monitoring, anti-poaching measures, and community-based livelihood programmes are prioritized. Project Tiger has delivered notable results—India now hosts over 70% of the world's tiger population, rising from 1,411 (2006) to nearly 3,167 (2022). It has also strengthened wildlife forensics, camera-trap monitoring, and landscape connectivity through initiatives like the M-STrIPES monitoring system. The project plays a critical role in protecting broader ecosystems, benefiting countless species and ensuring ecological stability.

Project Elephant, launched in 1992, seeks to conserve elephants, secure their habitats, and manage human–elephant conflict, a major ecological and social challenge. It prioritizes habitat protection, mitigation of conflict, scientific population monitoring, and welfare of captive elephants. Key interventions include the notification and protection of Elephant Reserves, management of migratory corridors, restoration of traditional elephant pathways, and reducing linear fragmentations caused by roads, railways, and transmission lines. The project has strengthened anti-poaching intelligence, deployed early-warning systems, and promoted community participation.

Project Snow Leopard, initiated in 2009, addresses the conservation needs of the vulnerable snow leopard, found in India's high-altitude Himalayan ecosystems across Ladakh, Himachal Pradesh, Uttarakhand, Sikkim, and Arunachal Pradesh. These regions are ecologically fragile and sparsely populated, making conservation uniquely challenging. The project adopts a landscape-level and community-based approach, recognizing that pastoral communities are essential partners in conserving high-altitude ecosystems. Its strategy includes reducing livestock depredation, promoting predator-proof corrals, involving local communities in monitoring, and developing climate-resilient management plans.

Project Snow Leopard emphasizes scientific research, including camera-trap surveys, genetic sampling, and habitat mapping. It supports the creation of high-altitude conservation areas, protects prey species like blue sheep and ibex, and promotes sustainable ecotourism. It is also part of the multilateral Global Snow Leopard and Ecosystem Protection Program (GSLEP).

Environmental education and awareness are promoted through the **Environmental Information System (ENVIS), National Green Corps (NGC),** and **Eco-Club Programmes.** Environmental education and awareness constitute a central pillar of India's environmental policy architecture. Recognizing that behavioral change and informed participation are essential for long-term sustainability, the Ministry of Environment, Forest and Climate

Change (MoEFCC) implements a range of programmes aimed at promoting ecological literacy, citizen engagement and youth leadership. Among these, the Environmental Information System (ENVIS), Eco-Clubs, and the National Green Corps (NGC) form the backbone of nationwide environment-awareness initiatives.

Launched in 1982, ENVIS is a flagship programme designed to collect, store, process and disseminate reliable environmental information to support decision-making, research, policy formulation and public understanding. The network operates through a decentralized architecture comprising ENVIS hubs in each State/UT and a series of ENVIS Resource Partners hosted by premier institutions, universities and specialized agencies. ENVIS contributes to environmental education in multiple ways. It develops thematic databases on subjects such as biodiversity, pollution control, ecosystem services, forests, climate change and waste management. These databases are made accessible through user-friendly websites, publications, newsletters and mobile applications. ENVIS also supports capacity-building through training programmes, certificate courses in green skills, internship opportunities and workshops for students, researchers and government officials. Its "Green Skill Development Programme (GSDP)" is a major initiative to equip youth with employable skills in environment-related sectors. Through digital outreach—such as the ENVIS portal, question banks, environmental quizzes and awareness materials—the system ensures that credible ecological information reaches teachers, students, NGOs, policymakers and the general public.

Eco-Clubs are institutional platforms aimed at nurturing environmental stewardship among school and college students. Supported by the MoEFCC and usually integrated into the State Pollution Control Boards (SPCBs) or State Nodal Agencies, Eco-Clubs engage students in participatory learning and practical environmental activities. The core philosophy is "learning by doing". Activities conducted under Eco-Clubs include cleanliness drives, waste segregation campaigns, plantation activities, water conservation practices, biodiversity surveys, anti-plastic campaigns, street plays and awareness rallies. Students are encouraged to adopt sustainable habits and spread awareness within their communities. Eco-Clubs also organize environment-themed competitions, debates, exhibitions and nature camps that instil values of conservation and responsibility. Teachers are trained as Eco-Club coordinators, enhancing the integration of environmental concepts with classroom learning. Through continuous engagement, Eco-Clubs cultivate environmentally conscious attitudes and leadership qualities in young learners.

The National Green Corps is a nationwide programme launched to institutionalize environmental learning among youth by forming Eco-Clubs in schools. Under NGC, lakh of school children—referred to as "Green Brigades"—are mobilized to participate in environmental protection activities. The programme develops a structured curriculum, activity-based modules and resource materials to standardize environmental education across schools. NGC strengthens community outreach by linking schools with local environmental issues and encouraging students to participate in district-level events, plantation drives, water harvesting initiatives, energy conservation campaigns and biodiversity conservation efforts. The programme emphasizes experiential learning, monitoring of environmental quality in local areas and problem-solving through youth participation. By nurturing eco-conscious citizens, NGC contributes to long-term environmental governance and grassroots advocacy.

In summary, MoEFCC's schemes collectively advance environmental protection, climate resilience, biodiversity conservation, and pollution control. They translate India's constitutional and international commitments into concrete action, forming the foundation of India's environmental policy and sustainable development agenda.

Importance of Environmental Impact Assessment (EIA) and Forest Clearance in India

Environmental Impact Assessment (EIA) and Forest Clearance (FC) constitute two of the most critical regulatory instruments in India's environmental governance framework. Together, they ensure that economic development does not compromise ecological sustainability, the rights of local communities, and long-term environmental security. Their importance has grown steadily as India faces rising ecological pressures–deforestation, air and water pollution, biodiversity loss, and climate change.

EIA serves as a preventive and anticipatory environmental management tool. Under the Environment (Protection) Act, 1986, and the EIA Notification 2006, it mandates that major infrastructure, industrial, mining, power, and commercial projects undergo systematic environmental appraisal before construction begins. Its core importance lies in guiding environmentally informed decision-making. By assessing likely impacts on land, air, water, biodiversity, and human health, EIA ensures early identification of risks and suggests practical mitigation measures. This helps avoid irreversible damage and reduces the cost of environmental remediation in the future.

A crucial benefit of EIA is its emphasis on alternatives analysis–examining more sustainable locations, technologies, or processes. This elevates environmental considerations to the same level as economic and technical factors. EIA also incorporates public consultation, giving local communities, especially tribal and marginalized groups, a platform to voice concerns related to displacement, livelihood impacts, resource access, and cultural heritage. This brings transparency, strengthens social legitimacy of projects, and reduces conflict between project developers and stakeholders. Additionally, EIAs generate baseline environmental data and long-term monitoring plans that feed into national resource management strategies.

On the other hand, Forest Clearance operates under the Forest (Conservation) Act, 1980, regulating diversion of forest land for non-forest purposes such as mining, roads, dams, irrigation, and transmission lines. Its importance stems from India's ecological dependence on forests—crucial for carbon sequestration, hydrological stability, soil conservation, biodiversity integrity, and livelihood security for nearly 200 million forest-dependent people. Forest Clearance ensures that forest diversion is treated as an exceptional measure, not a routine administrative process. It requires rigorous scrutiny of whether the proposed project genuinely needs forest land, whether alternatives exist, and whether the ecological loss is justified by public interest benefits. Mandatory compensatory afforestation, payment of Net Present Value (NPV) of forest land, and wildlife conservation plans ensure that the ecological losses are—at least partially—offset. The two-stage clearance mechanism allows detailed ecological appraisal, including the impact on wildlife corridors, endangered species, and landscape integrity. Forest Clearance is also vital for safeguarding tribal rights under the Forest Rights Act, 2006, as projects must secure Gram Sabha consent before diversion. This protects customary forest rights and prevents arbitrary displacement.

Together, EIA and Forest Clearance form the backbone of India's preventive environmental policy. They embed sustainability into developmental planning, ensure inter-generational equity, strengthen federal environmental governance, and uphold constitutional mandates under Articles 48A and 51A(g). While challenges exist—delays, quality of reports, and pressures for dilution—their importance remains central for balancing growth with ecological stewardship in a rapidly developing economy.

A key judicial body in environmental governance is the National Green Tribunal (NGT), established in 2010. NGT provides speedy and specialized adjudication of environmental disputes, enforces the "polluter pays" and "precautionary" principles, and ensures accountability of regulators and industries. Its judgments have shaped national policies on air quality, river pollution, waste management, and forest conservation.

Institutions dedicated to forestry and biodiversity include the Forest Survey of India (FSI), which assesses forest cover and monitors ecological health, and the National Biodiversity Authority (NBA), which regulates access to biological resources and ensures fair benefit sharing. Wildlife Crime Control Bureau (WCCB) combats poaching and illegal wildlife trade, supporting conservation enforcement.

Role of the Central Pollution Control Board (CPCB) in India's Environmental Policies

Central Pollution Control Board (CPCB) is India's apex pollution regulatory authority, established under the Water (Prevention and Control of Pollution) Act, 1974 and entrusted with additional powers under the Air (Prevention and Control of Pollution) Act, 1981. It plays a critical role in India's environmental policies by setting national standards, monitoring pollution, guiding State Pollution Control Boards (SPCBs), and coordinating nationwide strategies for pollution reduction and environmental protection. As a statutory body under the Ministry of Environment, Forest and Climate Change (MoEFCC), the CPCB is central to translating environmental laws into on-ground implementation.

A core responsibility of CPCB is formulating national standards for air, water, and noise quality. It prescribes National Ambient Air Quality Standards (NAAQS), categorizes industrial sectors by pollution potential, and defines emission and effluent standards for various industries. These standards form the backbone of India's pollution control regime, providing uniform benchmarks for SPCBs to enforce. CPCB also develops guidelines for waste management, hazardous waste treatment, biomedical waste, e-waste, plastic waste, and municipal solid waste handling, ensuring scientific and environmentally sound practices across States/UTs.

CPCB is India's principal agency for environmental monitoring. It operates large networks such as the National Air Quality Monitoring Programme (NAMP) and the National Water Quality Monitoring Programme (NWMP), covering thousands of monitoring stations nationwide. Data from these networks feeds into national policy, supports litigation in the National Green Tribunal (NGT), and informs major programmes such as the National Clean Air Programme (NCAP). Through Continuous Emissions Monitoring Systems (CEMS) and Continuous Effluent Monitoring Systems (CEMS), CPCB tracks real-time compliance of highly polluting industries.

Another major role of CPCB is coordination and supervision of State Pollution Control Boards. It sets guidelines, provides technical support, conducts training, and reviews SPCB performance. By harmonizing State-level actions, CPCB ensures consistent enforcement of environmental laws across India. It also resolves disputes between States regarding water sharing and pollution issues—reflecting its federal coordination function.

CPCB plays an active role in pollution control and enforcement. It inspects industries, issues directions under Section 5 of the Environment (Protection) Act, orders closure of non-compliant units, and imposes environmental compensation in coordination with the NGT. It identifies polluted river stretches, critically polluted industrial clusters, and non-attainment cities, enabling targeted interventions. CPCB's actions have shaped major national programmes like Ganga rejuvenation, industrial pollution abatement, and hazardous waste regulation.

In addition to regulation, CPCB contributes significantly to research, technical guidance, and innovation. It develops pollution abatement technologies, sector-specific action plans, and environmental modelling tools. Its technical reports guide national policies on vehicular emissions, industrial pollution control, water treatment, and waste management. CPCB also assists MoEFCC in drafting rules, policy revisions, and environmental notifications.

CPCB is also central to public awareness, capacity building, and environmental education. Through publications, real-time Air Quality Index (AQI) information, grievance redressal portals, and training programmes, it strengthens public participation and environmental governance.

In summary, the Central Pollution Control Board is the institutional backbone of India's pollution control architecture. Through standard-setting, nation-wide monitoring, enforcement, technical guidance, coordination with SPCBs, and scientific input into policy, CPCB ensures that India's environmental laws are effectively implemented and continuously strengthened.

Role of State Pollution Control Boards (SPCBs) in India's Environmental Policy

State Pollution Control Boards (SPCBs) are the frontline environmental regulators in India. Established under the Water (Prevention and Control of Pollution) Act, 1974 and later assigned responsibility under the Air (Prevention and Control of Pollution) Act, 1981, SPCBs play a critical role in implementing and enforcing the country's environmental laws at the State and Local levels. Their functions make them central to India's environmental governance, pollution control, and regulatory compliance framework.

A primary role of SPCBs is monitoring and controlling water and air pollution. They grant Consent to Establish (CTE) and Consent to Operate (CTO) to industries under the Water and Air Acts, ensuring adherence to emission and effluent standards. SPCBs regularly inspect industries, review environmental performance, enforce pollution limits, and take action against violators through penalties, closure notices, and legal proceedings. They also operate extensive networks of air and water quality monitoring stations that feed into national databases.

SPCBs are also responsible for implementing numerous environmental rules issued under the Environment Protection Act, 1986, including those on municipal solid waste, biomedical waste, plastic waste, hazardous waste, e-waste, construction and demolition waste, and noise pollution. They coordinate with municipalities, health institutions, industries, and local bodies to ensure scientific waste handling and compliance with prescribed standards.

Another key role is supporting the Environmental Impact Assessment (EIA) process. SPCBs provide expert inputs, conduct site inspections, and participate in public hearings for projects that require environmental clearance. Their assessments help ensure that project designs include adequate environmental safeguards, pollution control technologies, and mitigation measures before clearance is granted.

SPCBs undertake significant work in environmental monitoring, research, and reporting. They conduct pollution surveys, publish annual environmental status reports, and maintain real-time monitoring systems for highly polluting industries. This data supports evidence-based environmental policy at both State and national levels and feeds into programmes such as the National Clean Air Programme (NCAP) and Ganga Rejuvenation initiatives.

As enforcement agencies, SPCBs play a crucial role in compliance verification and industrial regulation. Through routine monitoring, surprise inspections, and laboratory analyses, they detect violations, issue improvement directions, and mandate corrective actions. SPCBs also support prosecution of polluting units and recommend action to the Central Pollution Control Board (CPCB) or the National Green Tribunal (NGT) when required.

SPCBs contribute to environmental capacity building and awareness by training industries, municipalities, and other stakeholders in pollution control technologies and regulatory requirements. They promote cleaner production, waste minimization, and adoption of environmental management systems (ISO-14001) across industry sectors.

In climate-related governance, SPCBs play an emerging role by developing State-level action plans on climate change, integrating air quality management, and facilitating cleaner technologies. Their local-level enforcement is essential to meeting India's national and international commitments on pollution reduction and sustainability.

In summary, State Pollution Control Boards are the operational backbone of India's environmental policy. Through regulation, monitoring, enforcement, waste management oversight, and community engagement, they ensure that national environmental laws translate into effective on-ground action. Their work is fundamental to India's goals of reducing pollution, protecting public health, and promoting sustainable development.

Role of the Ministry of Power in Environmental Policies of India

The Ministry of Power (MoP) plays a crucial but often understated role in India's environmental policy framework. Although primarily responsible for electricity generation, transmission, and distribution, its policies have deep implications for air quality, carbon emissions, energy efficiency, and the overall environmental sustainability of the power sector. As electricity production is one of India's largest sources of greenhouse gas (GHG) emissions, MoP's decisions directly shape the country's environmental performance and climate commitments.

A central element of the ministry's environmental role is reducing the carbon intensity of India's power mix. MoP supports renewable energy integration—working alongside the Ministry of New & Renewable Energy (MNRE)—through regulatory mechanisms, grid planning, and power sector reforms. The ministry is responsible for creating Green Energy Corridors, strengthening transmission infrastructure, and enabling large-scale renewable energy evacuation from resource-rich regions (such as Rajasthan, Gujarat, and Tamil Nadu). These measures make renewable energy more reliable and accessible, thereby displacing coal-based power and reducing emissions.

MoP plays a major role in environmental management through the Central Electricity Authority (CEA). CEA sets technical standards for thermal power plants, including norms on efficiency, water use, and emissions-related monitoring systems such as Flue Gas Desulphurisation (FGD) units, stack emissions monitoring, ash handling, and water consumption limits. These technical regulations, aligned with the Ministry of Environment, Forest & Climate Change (MoEFCC) norms, help India control SO_2, NOx, PM2.5, mercury emissions, and thermal pollution from coal plants.

Another vital responsibility is the promotion of energy efficiency, which forms the backbone of India's climate-mitigation strategy. MoP oversees the Bureau of Energy Efficiency (BEE), the nodal agency for energy conservation. Through initiatives such as the Perform, Achieve and Trade (PAT) scheme, Standards & Labelling Programme, and Energy Conservation Building Code (ECBC), BEE reduces energy demand across industries, buildings, and appliances. This reduces electricity consumption and subsequently cuts emissions from power generation. The Energy Conservation (Amendment) Act, 2022, administered under MoP, introduced Carbon Credit Trading, marking a major shift toward market-based environmental governance.

MoP also contributes to environmental protection by modernizing the power sector. Promotion of smart grids, smart meters, and digital load management enables demand-side control, reducing wastage and optimizing energy usage. The Revamped Distribution Sector Scheme (RDSS) aims to reduce technical and commercial losses, which indirectly prevents excessive electricity generation and minimizes coal dependency. Furthermore, the ministry's push for hydropower and pumped-storage projects enhances grid stability for renewable integration and provides low-emission alternatives for peaking power.

In addition, MoP has initiated a shift toward cleaner thermal power. The Ministry promotes supercritical and ultra-supercritical technologies, mandates ash utilization, and restricts old, inefficient coal units. It supports flexible operations of thermal plants to complement solar and wind power, reducing overproduction and saving fuel.

MoP also plays a role in electric mobility and clean transport by facilitating EV charging infrastructure standards, grid readiness, and electricity pricing frameworks. This forms an essential component of India's strategy to reduce vehicular emissions.

Overall, the Ministry of Power is central to India's environmental and climate-action agenda. Its policies on grid modernization, energy efficiency, renewable integration, emission regulation, and sustainable electricity access significantly influence India's transition to a low-carbon, cleaner, and more resilient energy system.

Role of the Bureau of Energy Efficiency (BEE) in Environmental Policies of India

The Bureau of Energy Efficiency (BEE), established in 2002 under the provisions of Energy Conservation Act, 2001, is one of India's most influential institutions in shaping environmental policy through the promotion of energy efficiency, energy conservation, and demand-side management. Though not a traditional environmental regulator, BEE's mandate directly contributes to reducing greenhouse gas emissions, lowering energy intensity, and helping India meet its international climate commitments under the Paris Agreement. By targeting energy demand, BEE complements renewable energy expansion and reduces reliance on fossil-fuel-based electricity, making it central to India's low-carbon development pathway.

A major contribution of BEE to India's environmental policy is through the Standards & Labelling (S&L) Programme, which assigns energy-efficiency star ratings to appliances such as refrigerators, air conditioners, fans, geysers, and industrial equipment. This programme shifts consumer preference toward more efficient products, reducing electricity consumption and curbing emissions at the source. It also encourages manufacturers to adopt cleaner technologies. Today, S&L is one of the world's largest energy-efficiency labelling systems and plays a crucial role in demand-side environmental governance.

BEE is also responsible for the Perform, Achieve and Trade (PAT) Scheme, India's first market-based mechanism for industrial energy efficiency. PAT sets Specific Energy Consumption (SEC) targets for energy-intensive industries such as steel, aluminium, cement, paper, power plants, fertilizers, and textiles. Industries that overachieve can trade Energy Saving Certificates (ESCerts). This reduces energy use and emissions from sectors that account for more than half of India's industrial energy consumption. PAT also complements India's carbon-market architecture introduced through the Energy Conservation (Amendment) Act, 2022.

In the building sector, BEE implements the Energy Conservation Building Code (ECBC) and Eco-Niwas Samhita for residential buildings. These codes influence architectural design, insulation, lighting, cooling, and Heating, ventilation, and air conditioning (HVAC) efficiency, ensuring that India's rapidly growing building stock is more energy-efficient. Efficient buildings reduce electricity demand from air conditioning and lighting, cutting emissions while improving thermal comfort.

In the transport sector, BEE collaborates with industry bodies for fuel-efficiency norms for passenger vehicles and heavy commercial vehicles, which lower fuel consumption and emissions. BEE also supports the growth of electric mobility through energy-efficiency norms for charging infrastructure and battery systems.

BEE plays a key role in the environmental aspects of India's power reforms by promoting Demand Side Management (DSM) and Smart Grid programmes. DSM measures–such as efficient street lighting, agricultural pump sets, and municipal pumping–reduce peak demand and eliminate the need to build additional thermal power plants. Through the UJALA scheme (led by EESL under BEE oversight), more than a billion LED bulbs have been distributed, significantly reducing electricity demand and preventing millions of tonnes of CO_2 emissions annually.

Importantly, BEE also acts as the national energy-efficiency knowledge hub, preparing energy audits, policy guidelines, national energy data reporting, and State-level energy-efficiency action plans. The annual State Energy Efficiency Index, prepared with NITI Aayog, fosters competitive federalism and encourages States to adopt environmentally sound energy policies.

Overall, BEE is integral to India's environmental policy framework. By lowering energy intensity across appliances, industries, buildings, and transport, it reduces emissions, complements renewable energy, delays the need for new power plants, and supports India's transition to a cleaner, more energy-efficient and climate-resilient economy.

Role of MNRE in Environmental Policies of India

The Ministry of New and Renewable Energy (MNRE) occupies a central place in India's environmental policy architecture as the primary institution responsible for accelerating the shift toward clean, non-fossil energy sources. Although established primarily for energy diversification, MNRE has become integral to India's climate change strategy, air pollution reduction, and sustainable development vision.

MNRE's role begins with its mandate to promote, develop, and deploy renewable energy technologies across the country. In an economy historically dependent on coal and oil, the expansion of renewable energy directly reduces greenhouse gas (GHG) emissions, curbs local air pollution, and mitigates environmental degradation caused by fossil fuel extraction and combustion. Its policies reinforce India's international commitments, especially under the Paris Agreement, where India has pledged to achieve 50% of its cumulative electric power capacity from non-fossil sources by 2030 and reduce the emissions intensity of GDP by 45%.

One of MNRE's most significant contributions to environmental policymaking is through the National Solar Mission (NSM), launched under the National Action Plan on Climate Change (NAPCC). The NSM triggered a rapid scale-up of solar capacity by promoting large solar parks, rooftop solar systems, and decentralized off-grid applications. This mission not only reduces carbon emissions but also supports climate adaptation through reliable rural electrification, reducing dependence on diesel generators, firewood, and kerosene. The mission's domestic manufacturing push—through schemes such as the Production Linked Incentive (PLI) for solar components—also fosters a clean technology ecosystem that aligns industrial policy with climate goals.

MNRE is also leading the National Green Hydrogen Mission, which aims to decarbonize hard-to-abate sectors such as steel, refineries, fertilizers, and heavy transport. By replacing fossil fuel–based hydrogen with renewable hydrogen, MNRE is directly reducing industrial emissions and supporting India's transition toward net-zero. This mission signifies a major strategic shift in India's environmental policy by linking industrial competitiveness with climate action.

Another major contribution of MNRE lies in the promotion of wind energy, biomass cogeneration, small hydropower, and waste-to-energy technologies. These programmes diversify India's clean energy mix and provide environmentally sound alternatives to coal and petroleum products. By facilitating biomass and waste-to-energy technologies, MNRE plays a role in waste management and reduction of open burning—an important source of particulate pollution.

MNRE's efforts in rural sustainability are equally important. Through initiatives such as solar irrigation pumps, biogas plants, clean cooking systems, and solar street lighting, the ministry helps reduce rural dependence on firewood and kerosene, thereby lowering indoor air pollution and deforestation pressures. Decentralized renewable energy (DRE) solutions also enhance climate resilience in remote areas by providing energy for healthcare, education, and livelihoods.

On the regulatory front, MNRE formulates policies on renewable purchase obligations (RPOs), green open access, grid integration, storage technologies, and transmission corridors that enable high penetration of renewables. It works closely with other agencies such as the Central Electricity Authority (CEA), Bureau of Energy Efficiency (BEE), and State renewable energy departments to mainstream environmental sustainability in energy governance.

In summary, MNRE plays a transformative role in India's environmental policies. Through large-scale renewable capacity expansion, mission-mode programmes, green hydrogen, and rural clean energy initiatives, it acts as a key driver of India's low-carbon transition and long-term ecological sustainability.

Role of the Ministry of Commerce and Industry in India's Environmental Policy

The Ministry of Commerce and Industry (MoCI) plays an increasingly important role in shaping India's environmental policy, even though it is not a traditional environmental regulator. Through its influence on trade policy, industrial policy, export promotion, quality standards, and investment decisions, the Ministry significantly affects the environmental footprint of India's manufacturing and trade sectors. As India moves towards a green economy and aligns with global sustainability norms, MoCI has become a key actor in promoting sustainable industrialization, circular economy models, and green trade competitiveness.

A major contribution of the Ministry comes through the Department for Promotion of Industry and Internal Trade (DPIIT), which frames industrial policy. DPIIT's policies now integrate sustainability as a core objective through initiatives promoting resource efficiency, green technology adoption, MSME greening, and cluster-level environmental improvements. Industrial corridors, manufacturing zones, and logistics hubs increasingly include environmental safeguards such as zero-liquid discharge, common effluent treatment plants (CETPs), green building norms, and waste-management systems. The National Industrial Policy (under draft reforms) emphasizes decarbonisation, green hydrogen, circular value chains, and renewable-powered manufacturing.

MoCI also influences environmental outcomes through standards and quality regulation. The Quality Control Orders (QCOs) issued under the BIS Act mandate environmental-friendly and safe product specifications. Restrictions on hazardous materials (such as chemicals, plastics, toxic dyes, batteries, and electronic components) support green manufacturing and prevent environmental dumping. By aligning Indian standards with global norms like ISO, IEC, and

EU environmental directives, the Ministry enhances sustainability in domestic production.

A critical area where MoCI intersects with environmental policy is trade policy and green global markets. With major export destinations–such as the EU, UK, and the US–introducing carbon border taxes, circular economy requirements, and extended producer responsibility rules, MoCI plays a central role in helping Indian exporters adopt cleaner production techniques. It negotiates sustainability clauses in Free Trade Agreements (FTAs) and works with industries to meet environmental compliance norms, thereby protecting India's export competitiveness. The Ministry also coordinates India's response to the EU Carbon Border Adjustment Mechanism (CBAM), promoting low-carbon technologies in sectors like steel, cement, aluminium, and fertilizers.

The Foreign Trade Policy (FTP) also incorporates environmental incentives. It supports exports of renewable energy equipment, organic products, energy-efficient appliances, green textiles, and circular-economy products. SEZs and Export Promotion Councils encourage cleaner production, waste minimization, and eco-label compliance. Several export councils now promote green certification, sustainable supply chains, and traceability mechanisms.

Investment promotion is another area contributing to environmental outcomes. Through Make in India, Production-Linked Incentive (PLI) schemes, and industrial FDI policies, the Ministry attracts investments in green industries such as solar PV manufacturing, advanced chemistry cell batteries, electric vehicles, green hydrogen, semiconductors, and energy-efficient appliances. These incentives support India's clean-energy transition and reduce reliance on environmentally harmful imports.

The Ministry also supports the development of green logistics by promoting multimodal transport, efficient warehousing, and reduced carbon footprint in supply chains. Policies under the National

Logistics Policy and PM Gati Shakti integrate sustainability through modal shift to rail and waterways, fuel-efficient logistics parks, and digital optimization.

India's Green Procurement Programme—spearheaded by the Ministry of Commerce and Industry (MoCI) through bodies such as the Directorate General of Foreign Trade (DGFT) and the Bureau of Indian Standards (BIS)—plays a growing role in steering markets toward sustainability. Green procurement refers to the government's systematic preference for goods, services, and technologies that have a reduced environmental footprint across their life cycle. Since public procurement in India accounts for 15%–20% of GDP, integrating environmental criteria has transformational potential.

The Ministry's efforts center on creating an enabling framework for sustainable product standards, eco-labelling, and trade policies that favor environmentally responsible production. MoCI works closely with the Ministry of Environment, Forest and Climate Change (MoEFCC) to strengthen the Ecomark eco-label, ensuring that domestically manufactured goods meeting eco-friendly criteria gain visibility in government and private procurement. DGFT has also incorporated environmental norms into export-import policies—for example, promoting energy-efficient appliances, restricting ozone-depleting substances, and supporting cleaner production technologies.

A key component is the integration of green procurement guidelines within procurement manuals, quality control orders (QCOs), and public tendering platforms such as the Government e-Marketplace (GeM). GeM now hosts a growing catalogue of eco-friendly items—LED lighting, recycled paper, low-VOC paints, biodegradable packaging, electric vehicles, and green office supplies—tagged with environmental attributes for easy selection by buyers. This creates market demand for green products, incentivizing industries to upgrade processes. Additionally, MoCI supports international commitments such as the WTO's Trade and Environment agenda, UN Sustainable Public Procurement (SPP) network, and G-20 resource efficiency frameworks. Through these, India aligns its trade and procurement systems with the global shift toward circular economy principles.

Overall, the Ministry of Commerce's Green Procurement Programme accelerates India's transition towards sustainability by using the government's purchasing power to create markets for green goods, drive cleaner industrial production, and promote long-term competitiveness in a low-carbon global economy

Lastly, MoCI fosters MSME sustainability through ZED (Zero Defect Zero Effect) certification, which encourages pollution control, waste reduction, resource efficiency, and clean technology adoption among small industries.

The Ministry of Commerce and Industry significantly shapes India's environmental policy landscape through green industrial policy, sustainable trade frameworks, quality standards, clean technology promotion, and global compliance alignment. By embedding sustainability into industrial growth and international trade, MoCI acts as a key enabler of India's transition toward a green, competitive, and environmentally responsible economy.

Role of the Ministry of Housing and Urban Affairs in India's Environmental Policy

The Ministry of Housing and Urban Affairs (MoHUA) plays a crucial and increasingly central role in India's environmental policy, especially as rapid urbanization intensifies pressures on air quality, water resources, waste management, land use, and urban ecosystems. While MoEFCC is the primary environmental regulator, MoHUA shapes the everyday environmental quality of Indian cities through reforms in sanitation, housing, urban planning, mobility, municipal governance, and infrastructure. As nearly 40% of India's population moves toward urban areas by 2035, MoHUA's policies significantly influence national sustainability outcomes and climate resilience.

A major contribution of MoHUA to environmental governance is in waste management and sanitation, where the Ministry leads the Swachh Bharat Mission–Urban (SBM-U). SBM-U 1.0 focused on eliminating open defecation, building toilets, and basic solid-waste management systems. SBM-U 2.0 shifts towards deep environmental sustainability through 100% source segregation, scientific processing of waste, bio-methanisation, composting, plastic-waste management, construction and demolition (C&D) waste recycling, and legacy-waste remediation. Large-scale landfill reclamation under the "Lakshya Zero Dump" initiative reduces methane emissions, groundwater contamination, and land degradation.

MoHUA also plays a key role in urban water and wastewater policy. The Atal Mission for Rejuvenation and Urban Transformation (AMRUT) 2.0 emphasizes universal piped water supply, water quality monitoring, 24×7 supply in select cities, and reuse of treated wastewater. Smart metering, rainwater harvesting, aquifer recharge, and rejuvenation of urban water bodies form part of its sustainability framework. The Ministry's thrust on wastewater treatment—through STPs, decentralized sewage treatment, and reuse for industrial and landscaping purposes—reduces river pollution and supports India's commitments under the National Water Policy and the Swachh Bharat Mission.

In urban planning, MoHUA guides Master Plans, Land Use Planning, and Transit-Oriented Development (TOD) models. These frameworks promote compact cities, reduced travel distances, green buildings, mixed-use zoning, protection of urban green spaces, and climate-responsive design. The Urban and Regional Development Plans Formulation and Implementation (URDPFI) guidelines incorporate sustainability, environmental impact assessments at the planning stage, and greater emphasis on ecological buffers, wetlands protection, and green infrastructure.

MoHUA also influences environmental outcomes through housing and construction policies. Under the Pradhan Mantri Awas Yojana–Urban (PMAY-U) and the Global Housing Technology Challenge (GHTC), the Ministry promotes green construction materials, energy-efficient designs, prefabricated systems, and reduced resource consumption. The adoption of the Model Building Bye-Laws encourages rooftop solar, rainwater harvesting, natural ventilation, and other environmentally sound practices.

A major environmental function of MoHUA is promoting clean and sustainable urban mobility. Under the Smart Cities Mission, urban transport programmes, and metro rail expansion, the Ministry advances non-motorized transport (NMT), electric buses, integrated public transport, pedestrianisation, and digital traffic management. These interventions reduce vehicular emissions—the largest contributor to air pollution in most Indian cities.

MoHUA also leads climate-resilience initiatives, including city climate action plans, heat-action plans, flood-management systems, early warning systems, and nature-based solutions such as urban forests, green belts, and sponge-city models. Smart Cities have been made laboratories for environmental innovation through smart water, smart energy, air-quality sensors, and integrated environment command-and-control centres.

Additionally, MoHUA strengthens municipal governance, enabling ULBs to implement environmental regulations through improved finances, user charges, property tax reforms, and capacity-building programmes.

MoHUA is a key pillar of India's environmental policy landscape. Through sustainable sanitation, wastewater treatment, urban planning, green housing, clean mobility, climate resilience, and strengthened municipal systems, the Ministry directly shapes environmental quality in Indian cities and contributes to India's broader goals of sustainable development and low-carbon urbanization.

Role of the Ministry of Heavy Industries (MHI) in India's Environmental Policy

The Ministry of Heavy Industries plays a strategic but often understated role in shaping India's environmental policy. Its contribution is largely sectoral, focusing on greening the automotive, capital goods, and heavy engineering industries—sectors that are traditionally resource- and energy-intensive. While the Ministry of Environment, Forest & Climate Change (MoEFCC) leads overarching environmental regulation, Ministry of Heavy Industries interventions ensure that industrial policy aligns with sustainability, low-carbon growth, and clean technology transition.

A central component of MHI's environmental contribution is the promotion of clean mobility, primarily through the Faster Adoption and Manufacturing of Electric Vehicles (FAME I & II) schemes. These schemes provide subsidies for electric two-wheelers, three-wheelers, buses, and charging infrastructure, directly contributing to reduced tailpipe emissions, lower fossil fuel dependence, and improved urban air quality. Through localization incentives, MHI also encourages domestic manufacturing of EV components, thereby strengthening India's green industrial ecosystem.

MHI also influences environmental policy by promoting energy efficiency and clean technologies in heavy industries. It supports modernization of machine tools, incentivizes adoption of energy-efficient capital goods, and strengthens technology upgradation schemes that reduce energy intensity and emissions. Initiatives under the Capital Goods Scheme push industries to adopt low-carbon manufacturing systems, waste minimization practices, and advanced industrial machinery with higher energy efficiency standards.

The Ministry's work in public sector enterprises such as BHEL, HMT, and Heavy Engineering Corporation (HEC) includes mandating environmental compliance, integrating Environmental, Social, and Governance (ESG) practices, and transitioning to cleaner operations. Several CPSEs under MHI invest in renewable energy, supercritical and ultra-supercritical thermal technologies, pollution-control equipment, and in some cases, green hydrogen pilots—helping reduce the sector's carbon footprint.

MHI's policy framework also supports circular economy principles. By promoting domestic manufacturing of capital goods and reducing import dependence, it encourages efficient resource use. Additionally, its support for industrial R&D, waste-reduction technologies, recycling of components (especially in automobiles and engineering goods), and skill development indirectly reinforces national sustainability goals.

Institutionally, MHI works closely with MoEFCC, NITI Aayog, Ministry of Power, and MNRE to ensure heavy industry's compliance with environmental standards, fuel efficiency norms (CAFÉ norms), and emission standards (BS-VI). This inter-ministerial coordination ensures that industrial growth does not conflict with climate commitments under the Paris Agreement and India's Nationally Determined Contributions (NDCs).

In sum, the Ministry of Heavy Industries serves as a bridge between industrial growth and environmental sustainability. By steering clean mobility, promoting green manufacturing technologies, enforcing environmental performance in CPSEs, and supporting energy-efficient capital goods, MHI plays an increasingly crucial role in aligning India's heavy industrial sector with long-term environmental and climate objectives.

Role of the Ministry of Jal Shakti/Department of Drinking Water and Sanitation (DDWS) in India's Environmental Policy

The Department of Drinking Water and Sanitation (DDWS) under the Ministry of Jal Shakti plays a pivotal role in shaping India's environmental policy, particularly in the areas of water resource management, sanitation governance, groundwater protection, and pollution prevention. While it is not an environmental regulator like the MoEFCC, DDWS contributes directly to environmental sustainability by improving access to safe drinking water, eliminating open defecation, and promoting scientific waste management—activities that significantly reduce environmental degradation.

A major contribution of DDWS is through the Swachh Bharat Mission - Gramin (SBM-G). By eliminating open defecation, promoting toilet construction, and shifting rural sanitation behaviours, the department has helped reduce soil and water contamination from untreated human waste. SBM-G Phase II further integrates solid and liquid waste management, including greywater management, composting of biodegradable waste, and safe disposal of plastic waste—thus supporting a more circular and resource-efficient rural economy.

DDWS also drives environmental outcomes through the Jal Jeevan Mission (JJM), which aims to provide functional household tap connections with adequate quality water. The mission has strengthened water quality surveillance, village-level testing labs, and community monitoring systems. By promoting source sustainability measures—such as rainwater harvesting, groundwater recharge, watershed restoration, and protection of drinking water sources—the mission helps reverse environmental degradation, reduce extraction pressures, and improve rural hydrological balance.

An important environmental role of the department is ensuring compliance with water quality standards for parameters like arsenic, fluoride, iron, nitrate, and bacterial contamination. DDWS coordinates large-scale mitigation programmes for arsenic- and fluoride-affected regions, promoting safer water technologies and alternative sources. These interventions protect human health while reducing environmental risks from contaminated water bodies.

DDWS also contributes to environmental policy through capacity building and community-led environmental governance. Village Water and Sanitation Committees (VWSCs), trained and supported by the department, integrate local environmental knowledge with scientific standards. This decentralized model aligns with India's broader environmental policy emphasis on participatory natural resource management.

Moreover, the department's programmes significantly support India's progress toward SDG 6 (Clean Water and Sanitation), which is deeply linked with climate resilience, sustainable water extraction, and pollution prevention. DDWS works closely with the Ministry of Environment, Forest & Climate Change (MoEFCC), NITI Aayog, and State agencies to align rural water and sanitation infrastructure with broader climate adaptation and environmental protection frameworks.

Namami Gange, launched in June 2014 by the Ministry of Jal Shakti (earlier under Ministry of Water Resources, River Development and Ganga Rejuvenation), is an integrated conservation mission for the Ganga River with a budget outlay of ₹20,000 crore, extended to ₹22,500 crore for 2023-26. It pursues twin objectives of pollution abatement, conservation, and rejuvenation of the National River Ganga through a basin-wide approach, ensuring "Aviral" (continuous) and "Nirmal" (clean) flows while promoting ecological integrity.

Key Pillars and Interventions

The programme rests on eight pillars: sewerage treatment infrastructure (e.g., new STPs creating over 5,000 MLD capacity), river surface cleaning, biodiversity conservation, afforestation, riverfront development (ghats and crematoria), public awareness, industrial effluent monitoring, and Ganga Gram initiatives for rural sanitation. Implemented by the National Mission for Clean Ganga (NMCG) with State Programme Management Groups, it integrates entry-level (immediate impact), medium-term (5-year), and long-term (10-year) activities, supported by World Bank loans till 2026.

Achievements and Institutional Framework

Significant progress includes completion of 92 sewage projects, surface cleaning at 11 locations, and biodiversity plans by institutions like Wildlife Institute of India. The National Ganga Council oversees it, with tools like Clean Ganga Fund for public contributions and IT-based monitoring. Namami Gange complements DDWS efforts by addressing urban-river pollution, enhancing rural WASH convergence for holistic environmental governance in the Ganga basin.

Role of the Ministry of Road Transport and Highways (MoRTH) in India's Environmental Policy

The Ministry of Road Transport and Highways (MoRTH) plays an important cross-sectoral role in India's environmental policy because transport is one of the largest contributors to air pollution, greenhouse gas emissions, noise pollution, and ecological disruption. While MoEFCC is the primary environmental regulator, MoRTH shapes environmental outcomes through transport planning, fuel-efficiency regulation, green mobility initiatives, and environmentally responsible highway development.

A key contribution of MoRTH is setting vehicular emission standards, which are central to India's air quality management. The Ministry enforced Bharat Stage (BS) VI norms in 2020, among the strictest emission standards globally, mandating advanced pollution-control technologies in automobiles and significantly reducing particulate matter (PM) and NOx emissions. MoRTH also regulates on-road emissions through PUC norms, in-use vehicle fitness testing, and inspection & maintenance systems, directly influencing urban air quality.

MoRTH also drives the transition toward clean and energy-efficient transportation. It designs regulatory frameworks for electric vehicles (EVs), flex-fuel engines, and alternative fuels such as ethanol, methanol, biodiesel, CNG, LNG, hydrogen, and green hydrogen. While the FAME scheme is implemented by the Ministry of Heavy Industries, MoRTH supports it through enabling policies like EV registration norms, safety standards for batteries, retrofitting guidelines, and green mobility corridors. These measures accelerate decarbonisation of the transport sector.

Highway and road development under agencies like National Highways Authority of India (NHAI) and National Highways & Infrastructure Development Corporation Limited (NHIDCL) incorporates environmental safeguards mandated by MoRTH. The Ministry integrates environmental impact assessments, pollution mitigation plans, wildlife crossings, noise barriers near urban settlements, and compensatory plantation along highways (Green Highways Policy 2015). These steps reduce ecological fragmentation, soil erosion, and biodiversity loss caused by road construction.

MoRTH also promotes sustainable construction practices. The use of waste materials—such as fly ash, construction and demolition waste, and plastic waste—in road building is encouraged, supporting circular economy principles and reducing landfill pressure. The Ministry mandates soil conservation measures, slope stabilization, rainwater harvesting structures, and environmentally sensitive design in hilly and ecologically fragile regions.

In urban transport governance, MoRTH shapes road safety and traffic management, indirectly contributing to reduced congestion and emissions. Initiatives like Intelligent Traffic Management Systems (ITMS), highway toll automation (FASTag), and logistics efficiency programmes reduce idling time, fuel consumption, and vehicular emissions. The Bharatmala and Gati Shakti programmes streamline freight movement, reducing logistics-related pollution and improving overall environmental efficiency.

MoRTH is also contributing to India's climate commitments. Through decarbonisation strategies, improved fuel efficiency norms, the Vehicle Scrappage Policy (2021), and modernized public transport standards, the Ministry aligns transport-sector emissions with India's Nationally Determined Contributions (NDCs) under the Paris Agreement. The scrappage policy in particular helps phase out old, high-emitting vehicles and promotes recycling of materials with lower energy footprints.

In summary, MoRTH plays a critical role in India's environmental policy by regulating vehicular emissions, promoting green mobility, ensuring environmentally responsible highway development, adopting circular construction practices, and supporting national climate mitigation commitments. Its decisions significantly shape India's air quality, carbon emissions, ecological conservation, and long-term sustainable transport transition.

Role of NITI Aayog in India's Environmental Policy

NITI Aayog, established in 2015 as a successor to the Planning Commission, plays a strategic, coordinating, and policy-think-tank role in shaping India's environmental policy. Although it is not a regulatory body, NITI Aayog's influence is central to integrating sustainability, climate resilience, resource efficiency, and green growth into national development planning. Its role spans environmental planning, inter-ministerial coordination, monitoring of national missions, and fostering innovations in sustainable development.

A major contribution of NITI Aayog is its work in long-term environmental and climate policy planning. It prepares national strategies and roadmaps such as the Nationally Determined Contributions (NDCs) Roadmap, LiFE (Lifestyle for Environment) agenda, National Action Plan on Climate Change (NAPCC) updates, and various decarbonisation pathways. These strategic documents guide ministries in aligning sectoral policies–energy, transport, industry, water, forests–with India's climate commitments under the Paris Agreement. Through its extensive modelling and expert consultations, NITI Aayog helps the government adopt evidence-based environmental decisions.

NITI Aayog also promotes resource efficiency and circular economy policies. It has developed key frameworks such as the National Resource Efficiency Policy (Draft), sector-specific circular economy action plans for plastics, e-waste, metals, and construction waste, and a roadmap for reducing material intensity in the Indian economy. These initiatives push India toward sustainable consumption and production patterns, reducing waste, pollution, and ecological footprints.

In the field of energy transition, NITI Aayog plays a pivotal role by coordinating clean energy strategies, promoting renewable energy integration, and preparing national plans for green hydrogen, EV transition, and battery storage. It has co-authored major reports on India's energy scenarios, renewable energy financing, and sustainable mobility. Through the e-Mobility Programme, pilot projects, and policy recommendations, it supports a shift toward low-carbon transport systems, contributing directly to emissions reduction and improved air quality.

NITI Aayog is also heavily engaged in water sector reforms, which are crucial for environmental sustainability. It developed the Composite Water Management Index (CWMI) to rank States on water governance, promote efficient water use, and address groundwater depletion and pollution. It leads national programmes on Atal

Bhujal Yojana (groundwater) and supports river basin management reforms, thus linking water security with ecological health.

Another important role is promoting sustainable agriculture and land use, including natural farming models, soil health strategies, agroforestry expansion, and climate-resilient cropping patterns. These interventions reduce chemical pollution, enhance carbon sequestration, and improve ecosystem stability. NITI Aayog also works on desertification and land degradation neutrality, aligning national policy with global goals under the UNCCD.

NITI Aayog strengthens environmental governance through data, monitoring, and performance indices. Indicators like the SDG India Index, State Energy Index, and Aspirational Districts Programme embed environmental metrics, pushing States to improve clean energy adoption, water quality, waste management, and forest cover. This competitive federalism model encourages States to implement stronger environmental measures.

Additionally, the Aayog promotes multi-stakeholder collaboration by bringing together ministries, State governments, civil society, scientists, and industry for climate and environmental reforms. It facilitates global partnerships, helps mobilize green finance, and guides India's participation in global environmental initiatives.

In summary, NITI Aayog shapes India's environmental policy through strategic planning, climate governance, resource efficiency frameworks, clean energy transition, water reforms, sustainable agriculture models, and data-driven federal performance systems. Its role is vital in steering India toward long-term ecological sustainability and green economic growth.

Role of the Bureau of Indian Standards (BIS) in Indian Environmental Policy

The Bureau of Indian Standards (BIS), India's national standards body, plays an important indirect but increasingly significant role in environmental governance. Although BIS is not an environmental regulator like the CPCB or MoEFCC, it shapes India's environmental policy through standards that influence product quality, resource efficiency, pollution reduction, and public health protection. By setting scientifically backed norms, BIS creates the technical foundation for environmental protection across industries, buildings, consumer goods, and infrastructure. It mainly does following:

a. Setting Eco-Standards for Products and Materials

BIS formulates standards that reduce environmental harm by improving product durability, energy performance, water efficiency, recyclability, and safety. Standards for low-lead paints, low-VOC adhesives, pollution-free firecrackers, biodegradable plastics, safe drinking water storage tanks, sustainable packaging materials, and improved industrial processes help reduce toxic emissions and waste generation. These voluntary or mandatory standards support India's shift toward cleaner production.

b. Enabling Energy Efficiency and Climate Mitigation

BIS works closely with the Bureau of Energy Efficiency (BEE) to define testing protocols and performance benchmarks for appliances covered under India's Standards & Labelling Programme (refrigerators, ACs, fans, motors, etc.). By codifying the technical specifications behind star ratings, BIS indirectly advances national climate targets and reduces electricity demand from fossil-fuel-based power generation.

c. Promoting Sustainable Construction and Resource Efficiency

BIS develops critical norms for building materials such as cement, steel, fly ash bricks, concrete, and aggregates. Many of these standards promote environmentally sound practices—such as the use of fly ash in construction, recycled aggregates, water-efficient fixtures, and energy-efficient building components. This supports India's green building movement and encourages circular economy practices in the construction sector.

d. Water Quality and Environmental Health

BIS plays a major role in environmental public health through water-quality standards such as IS 10500 (drinking water), irrigation water norms, packaged drinking water standards, and treated wastewater reuse norms. These standards guide pollution control authorities, municipalities, and industries in water safety, preventing contamination from heavy metals, pathogens, and chemicals.

e. Standards for Waste Management and Circular Economy

The BIS develops specifications for waste segregation, compost quality, recycled plastics, e-waste recycling processes, secondary materials (scrap steel, aluminium, paper), and biodegradable carry bags. These standards help implement national waste-management rules (Solid Waste Rules, Plastic Waste Rules, e-Waste Rules) and support extended producer responsibility (EPR) frameworks.

f. Supporting Environmental Regulations Through Technical Benchmarks

Environmental laws–such as the Environment (Protection) Act, Plastic Waste Rules, Air Act, Water Act–often rely on BIS standards for defining technical criteria. BIS provides reference standards for emissions, noise limits, safety devices, pollution-monitoring instruments, and environmental testing laboratories.

g. Strengthening Consumer Awareness and Green Markets

Through the ISI mark, Hallmark, and new Eco-Mark–linked standards, BIS helps shift consumer markets toward safer and environmentally preferable products. Eco-Mark-related standards promote green procurement and create incentives for industries to adopt cleaner technologies.

BIS plays a foundational, system-wide role in Indian environmental policy by setting standards for clean production, resource efficiency, green buildings, waste management, water quality, and consumer safety. Its technical benchmarks underpin environmental regulations, strengthen compliance, and support India's transition to sustainable development and a circular, low-carbon economy.

Conclusion

India's environmental governance architecture is a multi-layered system in which ministries, statutory authorities, regulatory boards and technical agencies work in complementary ways to protect ecological integrity. At the Centre is Ministry of Environment, Forest and Climate Change (MoEFCC), which provides national direction, frames laws, sets standards, and leads major conservation and climate initiatives. Supporting this apex role, Central Pollution Control Board (CPCB) acts as the national regulator for pollution control–developing norms, monitoring compliance, advising governments, and coordinating nationwide programs such as NCAP, water quality assessments, and hazardous waste oversight. Other ministries–such as Power, New & Renewable Energy, Jal Shakti, Heavy Industries, and Commerce–embed sustainability criteria in their sectoral policies, creating a whole-of-government approach to environmental protection.

Institutions such as the Bureau of Energy Efficiency (BEE) and Bureau of Indian Standards (BIS) strengthen India's environmental policy through market-based and technical interventions. BEE drives India's energy-efficiency transformation through standards, labelling, energy conservation building codes, and schemes like PAT, thereby reducing emissions and resource use. BIS ensures product and process quality through environmental and safety standards, supports eco-labelling (Ecomark), and enables green procurement and circular economy objectives.

At the State level, State Pollution Control Boards (SPCBs) translate national policies into ground-level action. They issue consents to industries, enforce compliance, undertake inspections, monitor ambient air and water quality, and take legal action against violators. Together, CPCB and SPCBs form the backbone of India's command-and-control regulatory framework.

Collectively, these institutions form a coordinated ecosystem of policy design, regulation, technical standard-setting, monitoring, and enforcement. Their synergistic functioning is essential for ensuring that India's environmental policies are effective, science-based, and aligned with long-term goals of sustainability, climate resilience, and green growth.

India's environmental governance rests on a network of key Ministries and specialized institutions whose coordinated roles ensure that policies are implemented effectively on the ground. Each institution contributes a distinct regulatory, monitoring, or standard-setting function, creating a multi-layered system that addresses pollution control, resource efficiency, biodiversity protection, and sustainable development. Together, these Ministries and institutions create an integrated ecosystem where policy, regulation, scientific monitoring, and standard-setting reinforce each other. Their combined efforts are essential for safeguarding India's environmental health, enabling sustainable development, and ensuring that economic growth does not come at the cost of ecological degradation.

Chapter 3:

Circular Economy and Waste Management

The planet's resources are finite, so it's crucial that people, governments and companies work together to use them more responsibly. The traditional model where raw materials are collected and transformed into products that consumers use until discarding them as waste, with no concern for their impact on ecology and consequences. It prioritizes profit over sustainability, with products made to be thrown away once they've been used. Environmental impacts of today's "take, make, waste" or "linear" economy are extensive. According to UNEP, resource extraction has tripled since 1970 and it is projected to grow by another 70% by 2050, with the impacts of climate change, biodiversity loss and pollution being felt all around the world. Currently, global economy is only 8.6% circular. A rapid shift to a more circular economy, could dramatically cut resource use, and coupled with decarbonization, can deliver a low carbon and lower environmental impact future. A circular economy is a climate-resilient economy, there is very little waste and wastage and products and raw materials can be reused or repurposed. In a circular economy, people will be able to reuse nearly all products again and again. If a product is broken, it will be repaired. And if that is no longer possible, new products will be made from it. In a circular economy, waste is the new raw material. A product's life is no longer a straight line from being produced to being consumed and then discarded.

Differences between Linear and Circular Economy

No.	Linear Economy	Circular Economy
1	Take-Make-Waste Economy	Make-Use-Return Economy.
2	Short-Term Focus	Takes a Long-Term View.
3	Based on a Linear Flow of Resources	Based on a Circular Flow of Resources.
4	Has a Top-Down Approach	Has a Collective Approach.
5	Based on Ownership	Based on Access.
6	Involves Extraction and Depletion of resources	Involves Reuse and Recycling of Resources.
7	Follows a Linear path of resources	Follows a Closed-Loop Cycle of Resources.
8	Focused on Profit Maximization	Focused on Resource Efficiency and Sustainability.
9	Based on a Production, Use and Disposal	Based on a Model of Production, Reuse and Recycle.
10	Based on a Linear Model of Growth	Based on a Model of Stability.
11	Focused on Consumption	Focused on Production.
12	Has a Traditional Economic Model	Has a more Modern Economic Model.
13	Based on a concept of "Buy More"	Based on a Concept of "Use More wisely".
14	Focused on Short-Term Gains	Focused on Long-Term Benefits.
15	Relies on Finite Resources	Relies on Renewable Resources.

Source:https://cerclex.com/blog/from-a-linear-to-a-circular-economy-the-evolution-of-waste-management/

The circular economy can boost competitiveness, drive innovation and economic growth, and create jobs in new areas. This saves raw materials, the environment and reduces CO2 emissions. It stimulates innovation, new business activity and employment. A well-functioning circular economy doesn't only depend on the government and industry. Consumers, too, have a role to play and choosing sustainable products must become their new standard. Consumers also contribute to a circular economy by using things longer, repairing them or taking them to a second-hand shop. The government wants to stimulate this behaviour by giving the circular economy a place in education and by running public awareness campaigns.

As India advances toward becoming a $5 trillion economy, transitioning to a circular economy presents a multi-trillion-dollar opportunity, particularly in key sectors such as agriculture, electronics, automotive, construction, and textiles. India's Circular Economy (CE) policy framework aims to shift from a linear "take–make–dispose" model to a resource-efficient, regenerative system. Sectors such as automobiles, construction, electronics and textiles may gain strong benefits through material efficiency, eco-design and extended product lifecycles. CE fosters innovation in alternative materials, recycling technologies, modular design and circular supply chains. This enhances productivity and global competitiveness, particularly as international markets increasingly prefer low-carbon, circular products. CE directly addresses solid waste, pollution and emissions. By closing material loops, India can reduce landfill pressure, minimize plastics leakage into rivers and oceans, and cut air pollution caused by burning waste and crop residues. CE also supports climate goals by reducing lifecycle emissions across industry and transportation. With rising EV adoption, India faces a growing demand for lithium, cobalt and nickel. CE—through battery reuse, repurposing and recycling—can recover critical minerals domestically and support energy security. Similarly, solar panel recycling can help reclaim glass, silver and silicon, ensuring long-term viability of renewable energy expansion. In agriculture, circularity transforms waste into value through compost, bio-CNG, biochar and organic fertilizers. This reduces chemical fertilizer dependence, improves soil health, and offers farmers alternative income streams. It also mitigates problem of stubble burning and contribute to better air quality. Circularity can support cities through decentralized waste management, construction & demolition (C&D) waste recycling, water reuse, and circular buildings. Sustainable public procurement can create stable markets for recycled materials such as plastics, steel, aggregates and paper.

India's shift toward a circular economy gained momentum only after 2018, driven by resource scarcity, waste challenges, and climate commitments under the Paris Agreement. The approach focuses on designing out waste, keeping materials in use, and regenerating natural systems. India's policy landscape now embeds circularity across sectors through legislation, mission-mode initiatives, and market-based instruments. Mission Circular Economy is also a thrust area of the Government. Hon'ble Prime Minister in his address to the nation on the occasion of 75th Independence Day on 15th August 2021 highlighted focus on 'Mission Circular Economy'. The call of Lifestyle For Environment (LiFE) given by the Hon'ble Prime Minister envisions replacing the prevalent 'use-and dispose' economy with a circular economy, which would be defined by mindful and deliberate utilization. Development of circularity in different waste streams will not only have environmental benefits in terms of recovery of precious materials, reduced use of virgin material, environmentally sound management of wastes but also socio-economic benefits. Policies and programmes for unlocking the potential of Circular Economy will lead to creation of new job and business opportunities.

Implementation Strategies & Institutional Mechanisms for CE

To ensure transitions from plan to action, National Circular Economy Framework (NCEF) has been conceived and it proposes strengthening regulations & policies through mandatory frameworks, incentives, standards encouraging circular practices rather than linear disposal. It also aims at promoting public–private partnerships (PPP) to build infrastructure (recycling units, waste processing, material recovery etc.), financing facilities, and circular business models. Further, it also aims to establish coordination among different ministries, government bodies, industries, urban local bodies, and stakeholders via a shared roadmap. Another important aspect of it is to set up, monitoring, evaluation and data management – establishing systems for tracking progress, measuring resource savings, waste reduction, recycling rates, and environmental/climate impacts to ensure accountability. It encourages innovation – adoption of new technologies, material-efficient design, upcycling, repair, remanufacturing, and circular business models. Promoting circular procurement to encourage government and large organizations to prefer products made from recycled/recovered materials, thus creating market demand for circular goods.

NCEF and the sectoral action plans by NITI Aayog provide the overarching direction, focusing on reducing waste, enhancing recycling, and promoting lifecycle-based production. Ten identified priority sectors—plastics, e-waste, batteries, vehicles, construction, textiles, packaging, MSMEs, agriculture, and renewable energy—have defined CE roadmaps. The policy strongly emphasizes extended producer responsibility (EPR), eco-design, recycled material standards, and reverse logistics. Complementary rules such as the Plastic Waste Management Rules (2016–22), E-Waste Management Rules (2022), Battery Waste Management Rules (2022), and C&D Waste Rules (2016) operationalize CE principles. Initiatives like the Swachh Bharat Mission 2.0, Waste-to-Wealth Mission, and Vehicle Scrappage Policy reinforce implementation. Overall, India's CE policy aims to lower resource stress, cut emissions, create green jobs, and support sustainable economic growth. India's CE strategy aligns with Sustainable Development Goals (12, 13), Paris Agreement, and G-20 Resource Efficiency Dialogue.

NCEF 2024, is organized into two main parts. Part 1 defines a universal framework for circular economy across materials; Part 2 lays out material-specific action plans. Key guiding principles under Part 1 are: prevention, upcycling, recycling, and energy recovery– i.e. focus on lifecycle thinking, reduce virgin material use, retain value in products/materials, and recover energy where recycling isn't feasible.

It emphasizes resource conservation, waste reduction, and improved competitiveness of Indian industry through circular practices rather than linear consumption. Under Part 2, NCEF 2024, identifies 16 categories of materials/waste streams as priorities, and proposes tailored strategies for each. These include: municipal solid waste (MSW), domestic and industrial wastewater / liquid waste, scrap metal, e-waste (electronics), lithium-ion batteries, solar panels / pv waste, plastics & plastic waste, agricultural waste, Gypsum waste, Used oil, Hazardous and toxic waste, Tyres and rubber waste, End-of-Life Vehicles (ELVs) / automotive waste, Construction & demolition (C&D) waste, textile waste and other liquid/industrial waste streams. For each category, NCEF outlines concrete targets, policies, and pathways – to improve collection, recycling/resource recovery, safe disposal, reuse or repurposing, and use in new value chains. For examples, 100% segregation and recycling efforts for municipal waste; recycling/recovery of metals from batteries and scrap; reuse or recycling of solar panels; energy recovery or recycling of tyres/rubber; recycling of waste textiles; reuse or refinement of used oil, etc.

To expedite the transition of the country from a linear to a circular economy, 11 Committees were formed to be led by the concerned Line Ministries and comprising officials from Ministry of Environment and Forest Climate Change (MoEFCC) and NITI (National Institution for Transforming India) Aayog, domain experts, academics and industry representatives for 11 focus areas. The Committees gave detailed action plans for their specific target areas for transition from a linear to a circular economy. Circular Economy Action Plans for 10 waste categories (Lithium-ion batteries; E-waste; Toxic and hazardous industrial waste; Scrap metal (ferrous and non-ferrous); Tyre and Rubber; End of Life Vehicles; Gypsum, Used Oil, Solar Panels and Municipal Solid Waste have been finalized, and are under implementation. Respective Nodal Ministries (Li-ion batteries -NITI Aayog; E-waste - Ministry of Electronics and Information Technology (MEITY); Toxic and hazardous industrial waste - D/o Chemicals and Petrochemicals; Scrap metal (ferrous and non-ferrous) - Ministry of Steel; Tyre and Rubber - Ministry of Environment Forest and Climate Change (MoEFCC); End of Life Vehicles - Ministry of Road Transport and Highways (MoRTH); Gypsum - Department for Promotion of Industry and Internal Trade (DPIIT); Used Oil - Ministry of Petroleum and Natural Energy (MoPNG); Solar Panels - Ministry of New and Renewable Energy (MNRE); and Municipal Solid Waste - Ministry of Housing and Urban Affairs (MoHUA) are coordinating on progress of implementation of these action plans.

Recent regulations by the MoEFCC: Regulations mandating market based extended producer responsibility (EPR) on producers, importers and brand owners following the principle of circular economy have been notified by the MoEFCC, Government of India in the following four categories of wastes i.e., plastic packaging waste, battery waste, e-waste and waste tyre.

- Guidelines on EPR for Plastic Packaging on 16.02.2022.
- Battery Waste Management Rules, 2022on 22.08.2022.
- E-Waste (Management) Rules, 2022 on 02.11.2022.
- Extended Producer Responsibility (EPR) for Waste Tyre, 2022 on 21.07.2022.

These rules set out EPR targets for manufacturers, producers, importers, and brand owners, along with enabling transactions among stakeholders for Extended Producer Responsibility (EPR) certificates. The Government of India has come up with following policies as a part of its focus on building circular economy. Many other important Schemes have also been undertaken by the Government of India and are discussed below.

Swachh Bharat Mission (SBM) 2.0 (launched in 2021) builds on SBM 1.0 and explicitly incorporates circular economy principles to move urban India from waste collection to waste processing, recovery, and resource efficiency. Its core objective is not just cleanliness but turning waste into resources, thereby reducing landfill dependence and promoting urban sustainability. SBM 2.0 strengthens urban sanitation by embedding clear circular economy principles into waste management. Unlike SBM 1.0, which focused on eliminating open defecation and basic cleanliness, SBM 2.0 aims to reduce landfill burden, maximize resource recovery, and convert waste into usable products. It mandates 100% source segregation of waste to enable recycling, composting, and safe disposal. The mission promotes Material Recovery Facilities (MRFs) for sorting dry waste into recyclable streams, while composting and bio-methanation units convert organic waste into compost and biogas, supporting nutrient and energy circularity. The policy expands construction and demolition waste recycling plants, encourages reuse of debris, and integrates plastic waste management and EPR mechanisms. By supporting waste-to-energy projects, decentralized processing, and digital waste tracking, SBM 2.0 fosters circular business models. Overall, the mission advances urban sustainability by transforming waste into resources and creating green economic opportunities.

Waste-to-Wealth Mission is a key initiative of the Office of the Principal Scientific Adviser (PSA) to the Government of India, launched under the Prime Minister's Science, Technology & Innovation Advisory Council (PM-STIAC). Its objective is to transform India's growing waste challenge into an opportunity by promoting scientific processing, recycling, and resource recovery in line with circular economy principles. The mission supports the development and deployment of innovative waste-management technologies across solid waste, liquid waste, plastic waste, e-waste, C&D debris, and agriculture residue. It facilitates pilot projects, public–private partnerships, and technology demonstrations to convert waste into useful products such as compost, biogas, biofuels, construction materials, and recycled plastics. A major focus is on urban mining, decentralized waste processing, and creating a national repository of proven waste-treatment technologies. The mission also works with municipalities, industries, and start-ups to implement scalable solutions and improve waste segregation, monitoring, and efficiency. Overall, the Waste-to-Wealth Mission strengthens India's transition toward a circular, resource-efficient economy by turning waste streams into economic and environmental value.

GOBARdhan Scheme (Galvanizing Organic Bio-Agro Resources Dhan), launched in 2018 under the Swachh Bharat Mission (Gramin), aims to convert rural organic waste into valuable resources through scientific management of cattle dung, agricultural residue, and other biodegradable waste. Its core objective is to promote biogas and compressed biogas (CBG) production, reduce rural waste, and create an income source for farmers and panchayats. The scheme encourages the establishment of community and commercial biogas plants, CBG units, and slurry-based organic fertilizer production. By creating a market for dung and organic residue, it supplements rural livelihoods and reduces open dumping and burning of agricultural waste. The scheme aligns closely with circular economy principles by transforming waste into clean energy, organic manure, and bio-slurry. GOBARdhan operates as a convergence model, bringing together ministries such as Petroleum & Natural Gas, Agriculture, Renewable Energy, and Rural Development. It facilitates technical support, viability-gap funding, and market linkages for CBG sale through the SATAT initiative. SATAT initiative (Sustainable Alternative Towards Affordable Transportation) is a 2018 Ministry of Petroleum and Natural Gas initiative promoting Compressed Bio-Gas (CBG) production from waste/biomass. It aimed to establish 5,000 CBG plants by 2023-24, reducing import reliance, lowering pollution, and boosting farmer income. Overall, GOBARdhan promotes rural sanitation, renewable energy generation, nutrient recycling, and a sustainable rural economy.

National Vehicle Scrappage Policy: The Vehicle Scrappage Policy launched by the Hon'ble Prime Minister on August 13, 2021, is an important policy that promotes circular economy. The Policy envisages the creation of scrapping infrastructure throughout the country. The government plans to establish 450–500 automated vehicle fitness testing facilities across India as part of public–private collaboration through the voluntary vehicle fleet modernization programme. In addition to reducing pollution, the government's fleet modernization programme aims to improve road and vehicle safety, fuel efficiency, and the availability of low-cost raw materials for the auto, steel, and electronics industries. Private automobiles will be de-registered after 20 years if declared unfit or if not renewed. Although private automobiles will be eligible for renewal of registration after the 15th year based on fitness-test (valid up to five years), they will be encouraged to de- register their vehicles after 15th year.

The Vehicle Scrappage Policy may significantly reduce carbon emissions and air pollution while promoting employment and economic growth. As older vehicles are phased off the road, the service and manufacturing sectors will benefit from increased demand for new vehicles or electric vehicles. The Government of India has been focused on promoting the sale of electric vehicles through the National Electric Mobility Mission Plan 2020 and the Faster Adoption and Manufacturing of (Hybrid &) Electric Vehicles (FAME) Scheme.

Wet Waste Management: Scientific management of wet and dry waste is a prerequisite for developing sustainable cities and rural areas enabling them to reduce carbon footprints, become resources efficient and resilient. Scientific management of wet and dry is a key for operationalizing waste to wealth. The Solid Waste Management Rules, 2016, provide the statutory framework for solid waste management in the country including mandating separate processing of wet and dry waste by local authorities following the principle of circular economy. SBM envisions complete scientific management of wet and dry waste in the country.

Management of wet waste through generation of compost needs to be linked with the PM Programme for Restoration, Awareness, Nourishment and Amelioration of Mother Earth (PM PRANAM) which incentivizes States and Union Territories to promote alternative fertilizers and balanced use of chemical fertilizers. Further, Bio-methanation plants for wet waste management can be linked with the GOBARdhan (Galvanizing Organic Bio- Agro Resources Dhan) scheme.

Dry Waste Management Including Plastic Packaging: Dry waste is most valued stream of solid waste due to high economic value of recyclables. Municipal dry waste is nowadays sorted in Material Recovery Facilities (MRFs) to recover recyclables which go back to same manufacturing stream. The Ministry of Environment, Forest and Climate Change has notified guidelines for extended producer responsibility based upon market mechanism in order to drive growth of waste management sector in plastic packaging, waste tyre, e-waste and waste battery. Circularity in dry waste can decouple economic growth from consumption of primary resources. Other recyclable components of dry waste could also be included under EPR regime to push circular economy.

Extended Producer Responsibility for Plastic Packaging: The Guidelines on Extended Producer Responsibility (EPR) for plastic packaging vide Plastic Waste Management (Amendment) Rules, 2022, were notified on 16th February 2022.The Guidelines stipulate mandatory targets on Producers, Importers and Brand Owners for recycling of plastic packaging waste, reuse of rigid plastic packaging and use of recycled plastic content in manufacture of plastic packaging. The year-wise target for recycling of plastic waste across different categories of plastic packaging is given below:

Year	Target* (% of Extended Producer Responsibility)
2024-25	30-50
2025-26	40-60
2026-27	50-70
2027-28 onwards	60-80

* *Based upon plastic packaging category – rigid plastic packaging, flexible plastic packaging, multi-layered plastic packaging, and compostable plastic.*

Special Category Waste (E-Waste, Battery Waste, Tyre Waste): India is among the world's largest producers of electronic waste, driven by rapid digitization, growing consumer electronics usage, and shorter product life cycles. E-waste contains valuable materials like gold, copper, and rare earth metals, but also hazardous substances such as lead and mercury, which pose environmental and health risks if not managed properly. The data on E-waste, including collection, processing, and generation, is compiled by the Central Pollution Control Board (CPCB) under the MoEFCC, based on information from registered producers, recyclers, and authorized dismantlers. India generates approximately 3.8 million metric tonnes (MMT) of e-waste annually as of FY24, making it the world's third-largest producer after China and the USA. Recycling and processing of special category waste such as e-waste, battery waste, and end of life vehicles are linked with recovery of valuable raw materials, which can be further used as inputs for further manufacturing. Recycling of e-waste and battery waste leads to recovery of precious metals. Therefore, circularity in special category waste will lead to reduction in use of virgin raw materials and also reduction in imports of virgin raw materials not available in the country or not available as per requirement.

Extended Producer Responsibility on E-Waste: Under the E-Waste (Management) Rules, 2016, twenty-one (21) types of electrical and electronic equipment (EEE) have been notified. The E-Waste (Management) Rules, 2022 is a transformative step towards implementation of the announcement made by Hon'ble Prime Minister to promote Circular Economy in full earnest. Number of e-waste items covered under extended producer responsibility increases from 21 to 106. Further, in new rules the collection target has now been changed to recycling target and start from 60% of the quantity of waste generation as indicated in Extended Producer Responsibility Plan for FY 2023-24 to 80% for FY 2027-28 and remains 80% from FY 2028-29 onwards. The schedule for recycling target for E- waste is given below:

Year	Target
2023-24	60
2024-25	60
2025-26	70
2026-27	70
2027-28 onwards	80

Extended Producer Responsibility on Battery Waste: Ministry of Environment, Forest and Climate Change, Government of India published the Battery Waste Management Rules, 2022 on 24th August, 2022 to ensure environmentally sound management of waste batteries. New rules replace Batteries (Management and Handling) Rules, 2001.The Rules cover all types of batteries, viz. electric vehicle batteries, portable batteries, automotive batteries and industrial batteries. The rules mandate extended producer responsibility (EPR) on the producers (including importers) of batteries who are responsible for collection and recycling/refurbishment of waste batteries and use of recovered materials from wastes into new batteries. Producers (including importers) are mandated targets for collection and recycling/refurbishment of waste batteries in the range of 30%–90% depending on the type of batteries. However, the remaining batteries are also to be collected in 7-14 years' compliance cycle. The schedule for recycling target is given below:

Year	Target*
2024-25	55-70
2025-26	60-80
2026-27	60-90

**Depending on battery type– portable automobile, industrial, E-vehicles*

Extended Producer Responsibility on Tyre Waste: Ministry of Environment, Forest and Climate Change, Government of India published the notification on 'Extended Producer Responsibility (EPR) for Waste Tyre' on 21st July, 2022 through amendment in Hazardous and Other Wastes (Management and Transboundary Movement) Rules, 2016 to ensure environmentally sound management of waste tyres. These rules cover all types of waste tyre including tubes and flaps that is no longer mounted on a vehicle and is no longer used for its intended purpose. Extended Producer Responsibility (EPR) has been mandated on the producers (including importers) of tyres who are responsible for recycling/ retreading of waste tyre and use of recovered materials from wastes into reclaim rubber, crumb rubber, crumb rubber modified bitumen, recovered carbon black and pyrolysis oil & char. The schedule for recycling target is given below:

Year	**Target**
2022-23	35
2023-24	70

2024-25	100

Construction and Demolition (C&D) Waste Rules 2016 outlined the duties and responsibilities of multiple parties including waste generators, urban local bodies (ULBs), State & Central government Ministries and organizations. In order to make implementation easier, it also provided templates for the documentation required for each management phase. The goal of the (C&D) Waste Rules, 2016 is to make it easier for ULBs across the India to adopt good C&D waste management practices and ensure that recycled products find adequate and sustainable utilization.

As per NITI Aayog estimates, Circular Economy may give boost to Indian GDP by 4% to 5% by 2050 and India needs about \$50–\$80 billion investments over 10 years for full-scale circular infrastructure with an additional job potential of 10–15 million by 2040 in key sectors like waste, repair, bio energy, construction, etc. In India, currently, 62 million tonnes of municipal solid waste is generated annually, and only roughly 20% of this is processed or recycled. India's potential gain of \$2 trillion is expected from circular economy by 2050 (NITI Aayog). Policy Gaps in India's Circular Economy Journey is visible such as lack of centralized framework, no national law currently mandates circular principles across sectors, weak enforcement of EPR, compliance with EPR especially in plastics and electronics is weak, many small producers operate outside regulatory frameworks, inconsistent sectoral coordination (ministries such as MoEFCC, MoHUA, and MNRE run overlapping but fragmented programs), limited incentives for private innovation, India lacks green public procurement standards, tax breaks, or funding guarantees for circular initiatives, poor integration with MSMEs and informal sector, etc. The circular model depends heavily on waste pickers, recyclers, and repair services, and most of them operate informally. Apart from these, data deficiency is another concern as little standardized data exists on material flows, reuse rates, and sectoral resource productivity.

Circular Economy Policy Gaps in India:

Issue	Gap	Suggested measures
Reform Legislation	No national law	Enact Circular Economy Act
EPR	Poor enforcement	Digital tracking & penalties
Finance	Lack of tax incentives	Green bonds, subsidies
Informal sector	No integration	Formalization & training
Data	Scarce monitoring	Create material flow accounts

Private sector-led CE models in construction, mobility, packaging, and waste management can achieve break-even within 3–7 years, especially when supported by carbon credits and Corporate Social Responsibility backed initiatives. NITI Aayog has recommended enactment of National Circular Economy Framework Law, strengthen and digitize EPR Mechanisms, incentivize circular innovation with fiscal tools, formalize informal sector by developing CE Clusters and Eco-Industrial Zones, foster public-private partnerships (PPPs), build capacity among MSMEs and local governments, promote consumer awareness through labelling and education, integrate circular economy into School & Vocational curricula, etc.

The EU Circular Economy Action Plan (2020) includes clear targets for sustainable products, right to repair, and digital product passports. Countries like the Netherlands aim for 100% circularity by 2050. China's Circular Economy Promotion Law mandates resource use audits, product life extension, industrial symbiosis, large investment in eco-industrial parks supported by tax incentives. Japan has pioneered the "Sound Material-Cycle Society", with advanced recycling systems and consumer participation. Over 20% of total industrial input now comes from recycled resources. Brazil and South Africa Brazil incentivizes waste-to-energy and plastic recycling through producer cooperatives. South Africa supports circular start-ups via its Green Fund and skills training.

Country	Policy Strength	Key Tools
EU	High	CE Law, digital passport, EPR
China	High	CE Law, industrial parks
Japan	Very High	Product reuse mandates
South Africa	Moderate	Green Funds, innovation hubs
India	Low	Fragmented policies

Effectiveness of Environmental Taxes in Achieving a Circular Economy (CE)

Economic and market instruments promote circular economy (CE) by using price signals and incentives to shift behaviour from linear to resource-efficient systems. Extended Producer Responsibility (EPR) is the central CE tool, requiring producers to collect, recycle, and recover end-of-life products; it operates in plastics, e-waste, batteries, and packaging, creating markets for recyclers and reverse logistics. Eco taxes and differential pricing has the potential to discourage waste generation and the use of virgin materials. Deposit-refund system ensures high return rates for bottles, batteries, and consumer goods. Tradable certificates, such as EPR credits and Green Credits, create market-driven recycling incentives. Subsidies and viability-gap funding support recycling units, waste-to-energy plants, and circular start-ups. Green Public Procurement (GPP) generates demand for recycled products, while GST incentives can improve the competitiveness of repaired and refurbished goods. Together, these instruments strengthen recycling markets; reduce resource extraction, and support circular, low-waste economic growth. Environmental or "green" taxes on IT waste (e-waste) are typically designed as product or waste taxes that either increase the cost of environmentally harmful equipment, or fund proper collection and recycling through producer or consumer levies. No Indian laws impose a direct "green tax" (environmentally related tax on a physical unit of e-waste) on electronic waste. Instead, it mainly relies on regulatory frameworks with financial obligations like Extended Producer Responsibility (EPR) compliance costs and GST rates. Many countries, including India, rely more on regulatory "extended producer responsibility" (EPR) and compliance fees than on a straightforward per unit green tax on IT products. The E-Waste (Management) Rules, 2022 (notified under the Environment (Protection) Act, 1986) govern e-waste through EPR, requiring producers to register with the Central Pollution Control Board (CPCB), meet recycling targets (60%-80% of sales volume), and purchase EPR certificates from recyclers. Non-compliance triggers environmental compensation fees (priced at 30%-100% of liability), functioning as penalties rather than taxes. E-waste discarded by consumers or bulk consumers attracts only 5% GST when supplied to recyclers, while general scrap and e-waste processing falls under 18% GST, which critics argue that it discourages formal recycling. Recent GST reforms in 2025 lowered rates on some green technologies but not specifically on e-waste. Under India's E-Waste (Management) Rules 2016 and 2022, producers must meet annual recycling targets via registered recyclers and purchase EPR certificates, which effectively act as a compliance charge linked to the quantity of e-waste generated.

Environmental taxes—such as carbon taxes, landfill levies, plastic taxes, pollution charges, fuel taxes, and resource extraction taxes—are among the most important market-based instruments used to drive the transition from a linear "take–make–dispose" model to a circular economy (CE). Their core strength lies in internalizing environmental externalities by making pollution, waste generation, and resource extraction economically costly. They change the incentive structure for producers and consumers. One major way to increase resource efficiency is to levy tax on virgin materials, extraction, or environmentally harmful inputs, encourage industries to shift towards recycled content, reuse, remanufacturing, and material substitution. Countries like Sweden, Denmark, England, the Netherlands, etc. show that landfill taxes combined with recycling incentives significantly reduce waste-to-landfill and increase recovery rates, directly supporting CE loops. Environmental taxes also improve product design. Higher charges on waste or polluting products push firms toward eco-design, light-weighting, reparability, modularity, and durability. For example, the UK's Plastic Packaging Tax accelerated the market for >30% recycled content packaging. Such upstream design changes are central to CE. Another area where environmental taxes excel is behavioural change. Carbon taxes reduce fossil-fuel dependency and promote energy-efficient technologies; congestion taxes shift mobility patterns; and deposit-refund schemes for bottles demonstrate extremely high return rates. These behavioural shifts close consumption loops. However, environmental taxes alone cannot deliver a full circular economy. Their effectiveness depends on tax rates being high enough, stable over time, and complemented by infrastructure investments (recycling, waste segregation), regulations (EPR, bans), and innovation incentives. In many developing countries, low tax rates, weak enforcement, and political resistance limit their impact. Furthermore, taxes may create regressive effects unless revenue is recycled into social or green investments.

In conclusion, environmental taxes are a highly effective but partial tool for achieving a circular economy. When designed with clear price signals, adequate rates, and reinvestment of revenues into circular systems, they drive substantial progress. But they must be embedded within a broader policy mix to unlock a fully circular and regenerative economic model.

Way Forward

Transition to a circular economy is a very big opportunity for India and government has been proactive in formulating strategies and policies to ensure proper waste and resource management and leverage circularity principles not only to meet India's global environmental sustainability commitments but also to ensure that India has resources available to meet its growth aspirations. There are also concerted efforts to bring multiple stakeholders on the same page for policy implementation. Moving forward, it is essential to create an enabling environment for businesses to make circular practices profitable and businesses viable. It is also essential to emphasize on the importance of data driven decision making and the need for more research and development in the area of circular economy. Governments at all levels, from National to State to District, must work together to overcome the challenges of a circular economy. The government can introduce cheap financing channel and schemes like Production Linked Incentive (PLI) targeting circular practices adoption with clear objectives. Currently, most of the circular economy activities happen at the very end of value chains, resulting in sub-optimal economic and environmental outcomes. The authorities can help push the initiatives up the value chain through focused actions such as mandatory procurement of recycled content product in government tenders and clear targets and accountability for Extended Producer Responsibility (EPR) sector wise. State Governments and local authorities need to take steps for operationalization of waste to wealth through scientific management of wet and dry waste processing including plastic packaging, C&D waste, special category waste including e-waste and scrapping of end of life vehicles.

India stands at a critical juncture where circular economy adoption is no longer optional but essential. With mounting environmental stress, growing population, and urbanization, the only sustainable path forward lies in decoupling growth from resource consumption. The private sector has a significant role to play—through technology, finance, design, and entrepreneurship—especially if the government enables the right ecosystem. Drawing from global experiences and leveraging India's frugal innovation potential, a circular economy can power India's green industrial revolution, generate jobs, and strengthen long-term resilience. CE empowers rural economies through repair clusters, bio-energy plants, and cottage industries based on reuse and recycling. It aligns with traditional Indian practices of frugality, repair and repurposing. The circular economy holds vast potential for India—strengthening resource security, accelerating green growth, reducing environmental burdens, and creating millions of jobs. With the right policy push, financing and industry participation, CE can become a cornerstone of India's sustainable development strategy.

Chapter 4:

Market Based Instruments: Eco Tax in OECD Countries

The first important question is what could be rationale for levying eco tax when we all know that imposition of taxes leads to distortion in economic decision making. This distortion is also reflected into loss of economic welfare. However, this usually does not hold in the case of environmental tax, where market failures lead to inefficient decisions being made in the first place which taxation can help to correct. The main reason for levying environmental taxes emanate from 'externalities'. Environmental costs are not felt by the people undertaking environmentally-harming activities – as they are 'external' costs to society at large. These costs include global climate change following release of greenhouse gases (GHGs) into the atmosphere, as well as localized costs of pollution in various forms. When weighing up how much of a harmful activity to engage in, people will weigh up their private costs and benefits but because the external costs are not taken into account, too much of the activity is carried out from a social perspective. Environmental taxes can therefore be used to help people recognize the full social costs of their behaviour – to 'internalize the externality' – and thus reduce harmful activities to socially optimal levels, creating an overall welfare gain from taxation.

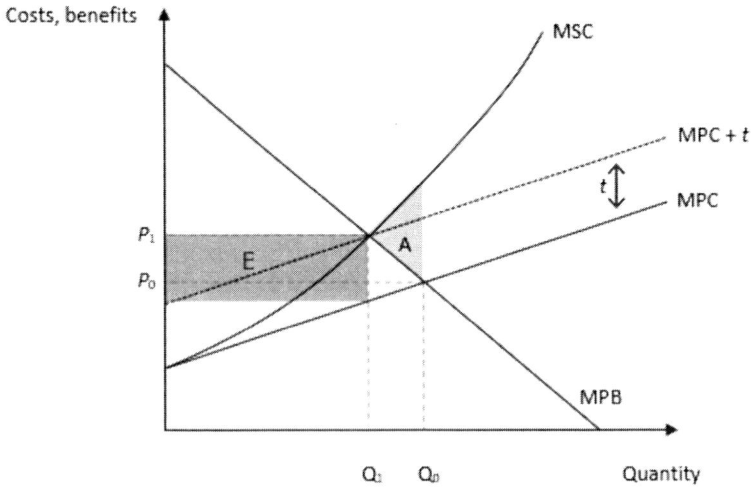

The idea mentioned in preceding para is illustrated graphically above. Imagine a firm situated in a small town deciding how much output to produce. In production of each unit of output, firm incurs a private cost to the factory, which is reflected in the upward-sloping marginal private cost (MPC) curve. As production levels increase, the additional cost of producing each unit gets larger as the firm has to run its capital more intensively and pay higher labour costs. The value to the firm of extra output is given by the downward-sloping marginal private benefit (MPB) curve. As output levels increase, each unit sell for a lower price. Taking a private decision, the factory will produce output level Q_0 and sell at price P_0. However, each unit of output produced by the factory generates a certain amount of pollution which imposes external costs on the residents of the town – health costs of pollution as well as the costs of noise and other disamenity costs associated with the factory's operation. At lower level of output, the additional external costs might be quite low, but as output increases, the marginal externality gets larger – the factory may have to run outside normal hours and pollution may only impose health risks once output exceeds a certain level. Based on the full marginal social costs (MSC, private and external costs combined) of its production, the optimal social level of output is lower, at Q_1, and should be sold at the higher price P_1. At the privately optimal outcome, there is a welfare cost given by the shaded area A. This is the total amount by which the social costs of producing output Q_0 exceed the benefits of producing this output. To obtain the optimal social level of output, the government can impose a tax equal to *t* per unit of output.

Environmental taxes are also referred as Pigouvian taxes, named after economist Arthur Pigou, are applied to correct market failures by internalizing external costs. For instance, taxing activities that produce pollution or negative externalities. Green taxes can be an effective tool in achieving environmental goals and addressing climate change by shifting economic incentives towards more environmentally friendly and/or sustainable practices. However, they should be carefully designed to avoid disproportionately burdening low-income individuals or industries and to ensure that the revenue collected is used for environmentally beneficial purposes. Green taxes, also known as environmental taxes or eco-taxes, are fiscal policy measures imposed by governments to promote environmentally friendly behaviour and address environmental issues. These taxes are typically designed to internalize the external costs associated with certain activities, products, or services that have negative environmental impacts. The primary objectives of green taxes are to incentivize individuals, businesses, and industries to adopt more sustainable practices, reduce pollution, and conserve natural resources. By taxing environmentally harmful activities or products, governments aim to make them less economically attractive while encouraging alternatives that have a lower environmental impact. While the primary purpose of green taxes is to influence behaviour, they can also generate revenue for the government. This revenue can then be reinvested in environmental protection initiatives, clean energy projects, or other programs aimed at mitigating environmental damage.

Rio's Declaration on Environment and Development urged countries to use "economic instruments" and to internalize environmental costs, framed through Principle 16 (polluter pays of the 1992 Rio Declaration). This heavily influenced popularity of Market Based Instruments (MBI) among countries and institutions and it can be framed along four axes: norm-setting, agenda-setting, institutionalization, and diffusion. Norm-setting came through the global acceptance of polluter pays; agenda-setting occurred via Agenda 21's repeated calls for economic instruments and subsidy reforms; institutionalization took place through UNFCCC and related regimes that later hosted trading and credit mechanisms; and diffusion happened as States and international organizations used Rio language to justify environmental tax reform, carbon pricing, and broader green fiscal policies. Together, these developments transformed MBI from relatively technocratic experiments into central pillars of environmental and climate policy worldwide.

As governments worldwide commit to reducing emissions and reducing environmental impacts, they are increasingly turning to fiscal policies to incentivize progress toward these goals. These taxes are designed not only to discourage environmentally harmful practices, but also to generate revenue that can be reinvested into sustainable initiatives and policy objectives. The landscape of green taxes is both diverse and rapidly evolving, reflecting the unique environmental priorities and economic conditions of each jurisdiction. This diversity presents a significant challenge for businesses operating across multiple regions, as they must navigate a complex and ever-changing array of tax incentives, penalties, and reporting obligations. As the green tax landscape continues to expand and evolve, the tax function and its stakeholders in other functions such as finance, legal counsel, procurement, supply chain and others will play a crucial role in ensuring that their companies not only comply with new regulations but also leverage them to advance their sustainability goals and achieve net-zero and other environmental targets.

Environmental taxes are a widely used tool to tackle climate change around the world. According to the World Bank (World Bank, 2022), in 2022 thirty-seven carbon taxes were implemented or planned to be implemented. Such taxes are usually considered as one of the best instruments to mitigate pollution, as they have two main benefits. Firstly, they allow people to internalize the externality by making them pay for the damage they generate (this is the polluter-pay principle), and secondly they provide fiscal revenue to governments. Yet, environmental fiscal policies do not impact agents in the same way; poorer households are more impacted both by pollution and by environmental taxation as they spend a higher share of their income on polluting goods and services. This is in contradiction with the fact that richer households are the ones polluting more (Chancel, 2021). In this case, pollution mitigation through carbon taxation works against inequality reduction and this leads to efficiency-equity trade-off. This link between pollution, carbon taxation and inequality, and the need to implement more equitable environmental policies has been highlighted in several Intergovernmental Panel on Climate Change (IPCC) reports and climate pacts.

OECD countries categorize eco taxes (also known as environmental taxes) and related charges into four main mutually exclusive tax-base categories: energy, transport, pollution, and resources with energy and transport dominating around 95% of revenues. These taxes target environmentally harmful activities to incentivize sustainable behaviour, generate revenue, and fund green initiatives, often measured as a percentage of GDP or total tax revenue.

Energy Taxes

This is most common eco-tax in OECD and it is charged per tonne of CO_2-equivalent emissions. Energy taxes apply to fossil fuels, electricity, and fuels used in transport, including all CO2-related taxes. Energy taxes, can vary greatly as they can be levied on the production, distribution, or consumption of energy sources, particularly fossil fuels like coal, oil, natural gas, and sometimes electricity. They are often aimed at influencing energy consumption patterns and behaviours, promoting energy efficiency, and encouraging the transition to cleaner and more sustainable energy sources. They aim to reduce consumption of non-renewable resources and promote efficiency. Examples include carbon taxes on greenhouse gas emissions and duties on imported high-energy goods. This is adopted by Sweden, Finland, Denmark, France, Canada, Japan, UK, etc.

Transport Taxes

These include taxes levied on import duty or sales taxes on vehicles and equipment, plus recurrent taxes on vehicle ownership or use. They address emissions from transport services and equipment. It is designed to reduce road congestion, emissions, and fuel consumption. Vehicle Registration & Ownership Taxes (green differentiated) based on CO_2/km or engine size and it is levied in France, Denmark, Netherlands, Japan, etc. Congestion Charges / Urban Road Pricing are another example and it is imposed in London, New York, Stockholm, Milan, Singapore (OECD partner). Aviation charges are levied for aircraft landing, and it is based on NOx emissions (Switzerland, Sweden) and Maritime Environmental charges as marine port pollution charges (Germany, Norway).

Pollution and Waste Taxes

Pollution taxes target measured or estimated emissions to air/water (e.g., SO2 taxes), ozone-depleting substances, wastewater discharge, and waste management like landfill fees or packaging taxes (e.g., plastic bags, batteries, tyres). These encourage waste reduction and cleaner production. Landfill Taxes / Waste Disposal Taxes are used in the UK, the Netherlands, Denmark, Sweden and their aim is to reduce landfill and promote recycling. The UK Landfill Tax is one of the earliest and most successful. Another example is Packaging & Plastic Taxes in Italy, Plastic Packaging Tax in the UK. They all target single-use plastics and non-recyclable packaging. E-Waste fees & Extended Producer Responsibility (EPR) charges on electronics, batteries, tyres and they are mainly used in nearly all OECD countries through EPR legislation. Beverage Container Deposit-Refund Schemes are applicable in Germany, Norway, Sweden, US, Australia, etc.

Resource Taxes

Resource taxes focus on extraction or use of natural assets, such as water abstraction, forestry products, hunting/fishing licenses, and mining royalties (e.g., sand, gravel). Mineral & Quarrying Taxes in form of aggregates levy in the UK and Norway, Australia have mineral extraction taxes to reflect environmental cost. Water Abstraction Charges for Pay-for-use system is used in France, Denmark, Spain, Holland. Forest use or Timber extraction fee is applied in Finland, Sweden, Canada (provinces), etc.

Eco tax in various OECD Countries

Norway is regarded as a global pioneer in environmental taxation, especially carbon, petroleum and waste-related taxes. Norway's eco tax milestones starts from the 1930s with early fuel duties evolving into targeted environmental levies, accelerating in the 1970s and 1990s to address pollution, emissions, and resource use under the polluter-pays principle. These align with OECD categories like energy, pollution, transport, and resources, with revenues peaking at 9% of total taxes in 1994.

Year	Policy Type	Description
1931	Energy/Transport	Petrol tax introduced, later differentiated by lead content (1986).
1971	Pollution	Sulphur tax on mineral oil.
1974-1993	Resource/Waste	Tax on non-refillable beverage containers, replaced by broader packaging tax.
1988-1998	Pollution/Resource	Tax on nitrogen and phosphorus in mineral fertilizers.
1991	Energy/Pollution	CO2 tax on gasoline, mineral oils, fossil fuels, coal/coke, and offshore petroleum emissions.
1992-2002(revived later)	Energy	CO2 tax on coal and coke.
1998	Pollution	Tax on pesticides.
2000	Energy	Excise duty on mineral oils (fuel oils, kerosene).
2003	Pollution	Taxes on HFCs and PFCs at ~180 NOK per tonne CO2 equivalents.
2005	Energy/Pollution(ETS)	Joins EU ETS for stationary plants.
2007	Pollution	NOx emissions tax at 15 NOK per kg, targeting key sectors.
2012	Energy/Pollution (ETS)	EU ETS extended to aviation.
2022	Pollution	CO2 tax on waste incineration at NOK 590 per tonne CO2-eq, rising to 2,000 by 2030.
2024	Energy/Pollution (ETS)	EU ETS covers maritime sector.
2027 (Planned)	Energy/Pollution (ETS)	EU ETS 2 for buildings and road transport.

Source: Norwegian Finance Ministry, ETS: Emission Trading System

Norway's environmental taxes (eco taxes) as a share of GDP rose from 3.0% in 1991 to a peak of 3.7% in 1996 and then declined to around 2.8% by 2007 and further to 1.98% in 2020, reflecting stabilization in post-revenue growth and ETS integration. A declining share of eco-taxes in GDP does not necessarily mean that environmental taxation is getting weaker – it could simply reflect economic growth outpacing tax base growth, or structural shifts (e.g. decarbonization) reducing taxable bases. This trend aligns with OECD patterns, where eco taxes averaged around 2% of GDP. As economies decarbonize, or as consumption patterns shift (e.g. less fossil fuel consumption, more efficient energy use), bases for many eco-taxes shrink. For example, reduced petrol/diesel consumption (due to efficiency, EV adoption, alternative modes) means less revenue from fuel excise taxes, which have historically been a major source of environmental tax revenue. In Norway's case, with high share of renewable in electricity, some of the traditional "energy taxes" linked to fossil-based energy use may lose base over time, resulting in reduced revenue.

United Kingdom does not have a single, universal "green tax" but a system of environmental taxes and levies aimed at discouraging pollution and encouraging sustainable practices. These measures fall under a broader environmental taxation framework that operates on the "polluter pays" principle.

Key environmental taxes in the UK include:

- Fuel Duty: This is a major component of environmental tax revenue, levied on petrol and diesel for transport, encouraging the reduction of fuel consumption and associated emissions.
- Air Passenger Duty (APD): A tax on the carriage of passengers from the UK airport, designed to address the environmental impact of air travel.

- Landfill Tax: Introduced in the UK as environmental tax, this duty is placed on waste disposed of in landfill sites to encourage waste reduction, recycling, and alternative waste management methods.
- Climate Change Levy (CCL): An energy tax applied to businesses on their electricity and gas supplies to encourage energy efficiency and reduce carbon emissions. The United Kingdom's climate change levy (CCL) was announced in 1999, legislated in 2000 and finally adopted in April 2001. The CCL is a tax on energy use, which embraces the supply of specified energy products as fuel used by business consumers in industry, commerce, agriculture and public administration.
- Plastic Packaging Tax (PPT): Introduced in April 2022, this tax applies to plastic packaging manufactured in or imported into the UK that contains less than 30% recycled plastic, with the goal of stimulating the use of recycled materials. PPT is designed to encourage the use of more recycled plastic and applies to plastic packaging produced in, or imported into the UK that does not contain at least 30% recycled plastic. An estimated 20,000 businesses across a broad range of sectors will be affected, impacting businesses operating in the consumer goods, food and beverage and manufacturing industries. Both manufacturers and importers of plastic packaging will be affected by PPT.
- Aggregates Levy: A tax on the commercial exploitation of aggregates (e.g., sand, gravel, rock) to encourage the use of recycled alternatives.
- UK Emissions Trading Scheme (UK ETS): This is a cap-and-trade system for energy-intensive industries, aviation, and power generation sectors. It sets a limit on carbon emissions, and participating companies can buy and sell allowances, incentivizing the shift to cleaner energy sources.

Key green taxes and initiatives in the UK in 2022

- Plastic Packaging Tax**:** This tax came into effect on April 1, 2022. It applies to plastic packaging that contains less than 30% recycled plastic and is either produced in or imported into the UK.
- Energy Sector Levies: Green levies in the energy sector saw a substantial rise in 2022, reaching a record £8.9 billion, up from £6.5 billion in 2021.
- Capital Allowances: The UK government announced its intention to reform the capital allowances regime, a move widely seen as a way to significantly incentivize companies to make sustainable, green investments.
- UK Emissions Trading Scheme (UK ETS): Following the Brexit, the UK implemented its own emissions trading system in January 2021, a key policy for pricing carbon emissions.

Landfill Tax (LFT): LFT is a tax paid by landfill operators on the disposal of material at a landfill site. The tax is passed onto businesses and local authorities through the gate fee for disposing of waste at a landfill. The tax aims to provide incentive for the diversion of waste from landfill to other less harmful methods of waste management such as recycling and incineration. The tax is charged by weight. There are two rates: standard rate and lower rate. Lower rate is applied to non-hazardous and less polluting materials and standard rate is applied to all other taxable materials including all disposals at an unauthorized site. With effect from 1 April 2025, the following rates apply:

- lower rate: £4.05 per tonne
- standard rate: £126.15 per tonne

Aggregates levy is a UK tax on the commercial exploitation of rock, sand and gravel. It was introduced as an environmental tax to encourage the recycling of aggregate. However, in addition to applying to the quarrying industry, it often applies when aggregate is extracted in the course of an infrastructure project. Aggregates levy is charged at a flat rate of £2 for every tonne of rock, sand or gravel extracted, and proportionally for any amount under that weight. The majority of businesses or individuals that 'exploit' aggregate within the UK are required to register with His Majesty's Revenue and Customs (HMRC), the UK government department responsible for collecting taxes (like income tax, VAT, corporation tax) for aggregates levy. To be caught by the levy, the aggregate must be 'commercially exploited'. This is defined widely so that it does not require the aggregate to be used commercially or even exploited. Aggregate falls within this requirement when it is:

- removed from its originating site;
- subject to an agreement to supply;
- used for construction purposes; or
- mixed with another substance other than water.

So, aggregates levy will normally apply to infrastructure projects involving either the removal of aggregate from a project site, or its use in construction on the site. There is no general exemption from the levy when aggregate is extracted in the course of an infrastructure project. However, a number of exemptions may apply to infrastructure projects in limited circumstances. Aggregates levy can only be charged once. This means that any aggregate on which aggregates levy has already been paid does not incur further aggregates levy charges for each additional time it is 'exploited'. Aggregates levy will normally apply to infrastructure projects involving either the removal of aggregate from a project site, or its use in construction on the site.

Sweden resorted to environmental taxation with energy taxes in the 1920s. It levied a carbon tax in 1991 at Euro 22 per tonne CO2 and then gradually raising it to Euro 134 by 2025, targeting mainly fossil fuels like natural gas and coal while exempting EU ETS-covered industry. Energy taxes dominate comprising 1.56% of GDP in 2019 (below EU average of 2.37%), alongside pollution levies on Sulphur, NOx, and others like pesticide and fertilizer taxes. Total eco tax revenue reached 1.6% GDP and 3.8% total taxes in 2024, supporting emissions cuts, efficiency, and renewable under the polluter-pays principle.

Finland is using a broad and well-designed mix of eco taxes to steer behaviour and support circular-economy goals. It introduced the world's first carbon tax in 1990, signalling an early shift toward pricing pollution. Finland's eco-tax system largely centres on energy taxation, with CO_2-based taxes on heating fuels, transport fuels, and electricity that are regularly updated to reflect climate targets. It also uses waste and resource taxes, such as the waste-disposal tax (1997) and packaging and beverage-container charges, alongside vehicle taxes differentiated by CO_2 emissions. Finland applies several product-based environmental charges—including on pesticides, chemicals, and mining waste—to limit ecological harm. Over time, the country has aligned its taxes with EU climate directives and expanded carbon pricing to meet ambitious neutrality goals. Overall, Finland's eco-tax framework is characterized by early adoption, broad coverage, and strong integration with climate and circular-economy policy.

Denmark is one of Europe's earliest and most consistent users of eco taxes, integrating environmental charges into its fiscal system since the 1970s. Its framework is built around energy and pollution taxes, beginning with broad energy excises (1977) and followed by a carbon tax in 1990 and Sulphur tax in 1992, aimed at reducing fossil-fuel dependence and air pollution. Denmark is also a pioneer in resource and product-based charges, including differentiated pesticide taxes (1994), water-abstraction fees, and a comprehensive waste and packaging tax system that discourages land filling and incineration. A CO_2-based vehicle registration tax and green transport duties further strengthen behavioural incentives. Over the years, Denmark has used periodic green tax reforms to raise environmental taxes while lowering labour taxes, making eco-taxation central to both climate and economic policy. Today, with agriculture and industry decarbonisation accelerating, Denmark is moving toward a comprehensive greenhouse-gas tax covering hard-to-abate sectors, keeping it at the forefront of green fiscal policy.

Canada's Tyre Stewardship framework is an important example of how Extended Producer Responsibility (EPR) and recycling-based regulation can transform a difficult waste stream into a circular, resource-efficient system. Tyres are a major environmental concern because they are bulky, non-biodegradable, flammable, and prone to long-term leaching of toxic chemicals. To address these impacts, Canadian provinces have developed comprehensive tyre stewardship programmes–mostly administered through non-profit stewardship agencies mandated by provincial regulations. While each province operates its own system, the broad objectives, funding models, and compliance mechanisms follow a harmonized national approach.

The central pillar of Canada's tyre stewardship lies in EPR legislation, which places responsibility for the collection, recycling, and safe disposal of end-of-life tyres (ELTs) on producers, importers, and retailers. Provinces such as British Columbia, Alberta, Manitoba, Saskatchewan, Ontario, and Nova Scotia have established dedicated stewardship bodies–like Tyre Stewardship BC, Alberta Recycling Management Authority (ARMA), and Ontario Tyre Stewardship (earlier)–to oversee programme implementation. These bodies are funded primarily through Advance Disposal Fees (ADFs) charged at the point of sale on new tyres. The funds collected are used for ELT collection networks, transportation, processing subsidies, public awareness campaigns, and enforcement.

A key strength of the Canadian system is its province-wide collection infrastructure. Municipal depots, private retailers, auto-service centres, and scrap yards act as collection points. Tyres are transported to registered processors who convert them into a wide range of value-added products such as crumb rubber, mats, athletic surfaces, moulded products, rubberized asphalt, civil engineering fill, and tire-derived aggregate (TDA). This creates local employment and supports a circular economy approach where discarded tyres become raw materials for new industries.

The programme places strong emphasis on environmental safeguards. Illegal dumping, stockpiling, and unsafe burning are addressed through strict regulatory oversight and penalties. Provinces conduct audits of retailers, haulers, and processors to ensure compliance with reporting requirements, storage guidelines, and transportation standards. Many stewardship agencies have invested in digital tracking systems to monitor tyre movements across the supply chain, improving transparency and reducing leakages.

Another hallmark of the Canadian programme is its market development. Provinces actively encourage innovative applications of recycled rubber through grants, pilot projects, and partnerships with municipalities. Rubberized asphalt initiatives have gained momentum in British Columbia and Alberta, improving road durability while absorbing large volumes of waste tyres. Public infrastructure—such as playgrounds, running tracks, flooring, and community sports facilities—frequently incorporates recycled rubber supported through stewardship-funded incentives.

Public outreach is an integral component. Stewardship organizations run awareness programmes on the importance of proper tyre maintenance, recycling options, and the environmental hazards of dumping. Educational campaigns target consumers, schools, and auto-service sectors to reinforce responsible behaviour.

Despite strong achievements, challenges remain. Market demand for recycled rubber fluctuates, affecting financial sustainability. Technological barriers still limit recycling of certain specialty tyres.

Moreover, programme fragmentation across provinces sometimes results in varying standards and inefficiencies. Efforts are ongoing to enhance harmonization, strengthen EPR compliance, and integrate circular-economy principles more deeply into tyre product design and end-use markets.

Overall, Canada's tyre stewardship programme stands out as a mature, robust, and evolving model. It demonstrates how legislated EPR, industry accountability, stable funding, and market development can turn a high-risk waste product into an opportunity for environmental protection, resource recovery, and green innovation.

Australia's Tyre Stewardship (TSA) Programme is a national, industry-led initiative, designed to improve the management of end-of-life tyres (ELTs) and promote circular-economy outcomes. Established in 2013 under the Tyre Stewardship Australia organization, the scheme operates as a voluntary product stewardship programme supported by tyre manufacturers, importers, retailers, recyclers, and fleet operators. It aims to reduce illegal dumping and stockpiling, increase domestic recycling, and support markets for tyre-derived products.

TSA accredits participants across the supply chain and enforces environmentally sound collection, transport, and processing standards. A key feature is its market development fund, which finances research, infrastructure, and innovation—including uses such as crumb rubber for roads, civil engineering, playgrounds, and manufacturing. The programme also supports export regulation and promotes responsible overseas processing.

Overall, Australia's tyre stewardship framework strengthens accountability, reduces environmental risks, and expands sustainable markets for recovered tyre materials.

Market-based instruments (MBI) form a central pillar of the **United States'** environmental policy framework, reflecting the country's strong preference for economic incentives over command-and-control regulation. MBI aim to internalize environmental externalities by aligning private economic decisions with public environmental goals, allowing firms and individuals to choose the most cost-effective pathway to reduce pollution. Over the past four decades, the U.S. has become a global leader in designing, piloting, and scaling MBI across air quality management, climate policy, water pollution control, hazardous waste management, and conservation.

The earliest and most influential example is the Acid Rain Program (ARP) introduced under the 1990 Clean Air Act Amendments. This landmark initiative created the world's first large-scale cap-and-trade system, targeting Sulphur dioxide (SO_2) emissions from power plants. By setting a declining cap and allowing regulated entities to trade emission allowances, the programme achieved a dramatic reduction in SO_2 emissions–over 50% within two decades–at compliance costs far lower than anticipated. The success of ARP established emissions trading as a credible environmental tool, inspiring later carbon markets worldwide.

Carbon markets and energy-related MBI expanded at regional levels. The Regional Greenhouse Gas Initiative (RGGI) in the North-eastern U.S. is a cooperative, multi-State CO_2 cap-and-trade programme covering the power sector. RGGI auctions emissions allowances and reinvests revenues into energy efficiency, renewable energy, and climate adaptation. Studies show that RGGI States have experienced faster emissions reductions and economic growth relative to non-RGGI states, demonstrating how MBI can simultaneously improve environmental quality and stimulate green innovation. Similarly, California's economy-wide Cap-and-Trade Programme, launched under its Global Warming Solutions Act (AB 32), has become the largest carbon market in North America. It covers electricity, industry, and transportation fuels, and integrates offset programmes for forests and agriculture.

Pollution taxes and fees are another significant MBI category. While the U.S. does not have a federal carbon tax, numerous economic instruments exist across sectors. These include taxes on petroleum products, congestion pricing in major cities, hazardous waste disposal fees under the Resource Conservation and Recovery Act (RCRA), effluent charges for wastewater treatment, and user fees for national parks. Many States also impose fees on landfill disposal and electronic waste recycling, discouraging unsustainable waste practices while funding environmental remediation.

The U.S. also employs innovative market-based conservation instruments. The wetland mitigation banking system, under the Clean Water Act, allows developers to compensate for unavoidable wetland impacts by purchasing credits from restored or conserved wetlands. This creates financial incentives for private ecological restoration. Similarly, habitat conservation banks support endangered species protection by allowing landowners to earn tradable credits for restoring critical habitats. These mechanisms harness market forces to expand conservation outcomes beyond government-funded programmes.

In water management, the U.S. has experimented with water quality trading, where point sources such as wastewater treatment plants can meet regulatory limits by purchasing pollution-reduction credits from agricultural or upstream sources. Although still evolving, these programmes lower compliance costs and encourage landscape-level watershed improvements.

Overall, the American experience shows that MBI can deliver cost-effective, flexible, and innovation-friendly environmental protection. While challenges persist–such as ensuring equity, preventing market manipulation, and harmonizing States and federal policies–MBI remain an indispensable component of the United States' environmental governance toolkit, balancing ecological sustainability with economic efficiency.

New Zealand is widely regarded as a global leader in using MBI to address environmental challenges. Owing to its high dependence on natural resources, strong regulatory institutions, and commitment to ecological sustainability, the country has incorporated pricing mechanisms, tradable rights, and incentive-based systems into climate policy, fisheries management, water governance, biodiversity protection and waste reduction. Collectively, these instruments help internalize environmental costs and align economic behaviour with ecological goals.

The most prominent MBI is the New Zealand Emissions Trading Scheme (NZ ETS), introduced in 2008. It is one of the world's earliest and most comprehensive cap-and-trade programmes. The system covers almost all major sectors—electricity, transport fuels, industry, waste, and forestry. Firms must buy and surrender New Zealand Units (NZUs) corresponding to their emissions. The government periodically auctions units under a declining emissions cap. New Zealand is unique in integrating forestry into its ETS: landowners earn NZUs for carbon sequestration through plantation or regeneration, while deforestation incurs liabilities. This has triggered significant afforestation and driven investment in carbon sinks. The ETS has also encouraged renewable energy deployment, energy efficiency, and low-emission technologies by creating an economy-wide carbon price signal.

Another globally recognized MBI is the Individual Transferable Quotas (ITQ) system under the 1986 Fisheries Act. Facing serious overexploitation of fish stocks, New Zealand introduced a transferable quota market where the government sets annual species-wise Total Allowable Catch (TAC) based on scientific assessments. Fishers receive or purchase quota shares, which they can freely trade. This creates long-term property rights, incentivizing sustainable harvesting and discouraging overfishing. The ITQ system is credited with rebuilding several fish stocks, improving regulatory compliance, and establishing an efficient, market-oriented fisheries industry.

MBI also play a central role in water resource management. Under the Resource Management Act (RMA) and regional council frameworks, regions such as Canterbury, Waikato, and Hawke's Bay have experimented with tradable water permits and nutrient discharge trading. Water use rights for irrigation or industrial extraction can be transferred, allowing allocation to the most efficient users. In catchments where nitrogen limits are imposed to protect rivers and lakes, farmers can trade nutrient discharge allowances, enabling flexibility and reducing compliance costs. These instruments encourage efficient water allocation and incentivize farmers to adopt better management practices.

New Zealand has also developed several MBI for biodiversity and conservation. Biodiversity offsets require developers to compensate for ecological loss by funding equivalent restoration or protection elsewhere. Conservation banking, pest-control incentive schemes, and grants to private landowners help mobilize private investment for protecting native forests, wetlands, and threatened species. Payments for ecosystem services by regional authorities' support landscape-level conservation outcomes.

In waste management, MBI have gained momentum through the Waste Disposal Levy, which imposes a fee on waste sent to landfills. Revenue is used for recycling infrastructure, circular-economy initiatives, and community waste-reduction projects. Additionally, New Zealand has introduced Extended Producer Responsibility (EPR) schemes for tyres, e-waste, packaging, and batteries, placing responsibility for end-of-life management on producers and importers.

Overall, New Zealand's experience demonstrates that MBI can deliver cost-effective, flexible, and innovation-driven environmental protection. Although challenges remain—especially in agriculture-dominated landscapes and balancing economic interests with ecological limits—market-based instruments continue to form a central pillar of New Zealand's sustainability strategy.

Greece has increasingly embraced MBI as part of its environmental policy framework, particularly after joining the European Union and aligning with EU directives emphasizing cost-effective pollution control. Faced with severe environmental pressures—urban air pollution, waste management deficiencies, overuse of natural resources, and climate vulnerability—Greece has used pricing tools, taxes, tradable permits, and financial incentives to influence behaviour and promote environmentally responsible practices. These MBI complement regulatory mechanisms and help Greece transition toward a greener, more sustainable economic model.

One of the most important MBI operating in Greece is participation in the European Union Emissions Trading System (EU ETS). As an EU member State, Greece has been part of the EU ETS since 2005. Power plants, large industries, and aviation sectors in Greece must hold emissions allowances for their carbon output, creating a clear price signal for decarbonisation. The rising price of carbon has encouraged Greek energy producers to shift from lignite-based power generation toward renewable energy sources such as wind and solar. Revenues from auctioning emissions allowances are channelled into Greece's Green Fund, supporting energy efficiency projects, renewable energy expansion, and low-carbon infrastructure.

Greece has also adopted a range of environmental taxes and charges. The carbon tax on heating oil, air pollution taxes, and energy consumption levies encourage households and industries to reduce fossil fuel use. A landfill tax, introduced under EU pressure to address Greece's dependence on land filling, aims to make land filling progressively more expensive and shift waste toward recycling and recovery. Similarly, Greece imposes taxes on single-use plastics, plastic bags, and certain packaging materials to curb pollution and encourage sustainable consumption patterns.

The country uses Extended Producer Responsibility (EPR) schemes for packaging, electronic waste, batteries, end-of-life vehicles, tyres, and lubricants. Producers must finance collection and recycling, creating financial incentives to design products that generate less waste. These EPR systems have helped Greece improve its traditionally low recycling rates and move closer to EU circular economy targets.

Market-based water management also plays a role. Water pricing reforms, required under the EU Water Framework Directive, ensure that water tariffs reflect the true cost of supply, treatment, and environmental protection. Higher tariffs for excessive use encourage households, farmers, and industries to adopt water-saving technologies, especially crucial for Greece's drought-prone islands and agricultural regions.

In the field of renewable energy, Greece employs feed-in tariffs (FiTs) and feed-in premiums, which guarantee producers a stable price for renewable electricity fed into the grid. These MBI have been instrumental in expanding solar photovoltaic and wind energy capacity, transforming Greece into one of the fastest-growing renewable energy markets in Europe. Auctions for renewable energy projects—another MBI—ensure cost efficiency and transparency in pricing.

Greece has also introduced a set of climate-linked tourism levies—collectively referred to as the Climate Resilience Tax—to strengthen its capacity to respond to climate change impacts, fund adaptation measures, and shift part of the environmental burden onto the tourism sector. Tourism is one of Greece's largest industries, contributing nearly 20% to GDP, but it also intensifies environmental pressure through high water consumption, waste generation, coastal degradation, energy use, and emissions. At the same time, Greece faces growing climate risks, including heat waves, wildfires, floods, and coastal erosion. These developments created the need for a dedicated climate resilience financing mechanism.

The most important component is the Climate Resilience Fee (CRF)—a restructured version of the earlier "stay over tax." Implemented from 2024, the CRF applies to all tourist accommodations, including hotels, short-stay rentals, and resorts. It is charged per room per night, with higher rates during the peak summer period when climate risks are greatest. Luxury hotels and high-category resorts pay significantly more, reflecting their larger environmental footprint and greater capacity to contribute. Revenue collected through the CRF is earmarked for the government's Natural Disaster Response and Recovery Fund, which finances wildfire recovery, flood reconstruction, early warning systems, resilient infrastructure, and climate adaptation projects across the country.

The Tourist Occupancy Tax, which existed earlier, has been absorbed into the Climate Resilience Fee structure. While the previous tax aimed primarily at revenue generation, the new climate-linked version explicitly connects tourist activity to environmental vulnerability. It introduces "polluter-pays" logic in the tourism sector by assigning part of the cost of climate resilience to visitors, thereby reducing fiscal pressure on Greek taxpayers.

Another important instrument is the emerging Cruise Ship Environmental Levy, which responds to concerns about emissions, marine pollution, and congestion in major ports such as Santorini, Mykonos, and Piraeus. Cruise tourism has significant ecological impacts, including underwater noise, air pollution from ship fuels, waste discharge, and overcrowding in fragile island ecosystems. Greece has begun implementing port charges and levies linked to vessel size, environmental performance, and time spent at port. These revenues support coastal management, port electrification, marine conservation, and monitoring systems, while also incentivizing cleaner fuels and more efficient ship operations.

Across all these instruments, the objective is not simply taxation but economic signalling–creating price incentives that internalize the environmental cost of tourism. By making peak-season stays more expensive, these taxes indirectly encourage off-season travel, reducing pressure on water-scarce islands and vulnerable landscapes. They also push hotels to invest in energy efficiency, wastewater recycling, and fire-resilient building standards. Short-term rental platforms, which have grown rapidly and strained local resources, are also brought under the tax net, improving equity within the tourism economy.

The Climate Resilience Tax package also aligns with Greece's broader climate adaptation and disaster management strategy, as well as EU Green Deal commitments. With rising climate impacts–such as the deadly 2023 wildfires in Rhodes and severe floods in Thessaly–the taxes create a stable funding stream for rebuilding resilient infrastructure and protecting communities. Overall, Greece's climate resilience taxes represent a modern use of market-based environmental instruments: they raise revenue for climate adaptation, encourage sustainable tourism behaviour, and ensure that visitors contribute fairly to protecting Greece's fragile ecosystems.

Germany is widely recognized as a pioneer in using MBI to protect the environment, reduce greenhouse gas emissions, and promote resource efficiency. Its environmental policy framework blends regulatory standards with pricing mechanisms, taxes, subsidies, and tradable permits, making MBI a central tool for achieving climate neutrality, supporting circular economy transitions, and meeting EU environmental obligations.

One of the most important MBI in Germany is its participation in the EU Emissions Trading System (EU ETS). Covering power plants, energy-intensive industries, and aviation, the EU ETS places a cap on emissions and allows firms to trade allowances. Germany, with its large industrial base, benefits from this system by encouraging cost-effective emission reductions and accelerating the shift away from coal toward renewable energy. Auction revenues are channelled into Germany's Energy and Climate Fund, which finances renewable energy expansion, electro mobility, building efficiency, and low-carbon innovation.

To address emissions outside the EU ETS—such as transport and buildings—Germany introduced a national carbon pricing system in 2021 under the Fuel Emissions Trading Act. This system sets a gradually rising carbon price on petrol, diesel, heating oil, and natural gas. The aim is to encourage consumers and businesses to adopt cleaner heating systems, energy-efficient buildings, and sustainable mobility options. Revenues support climate-friendly infrastructure, public transport, and household relief measures, making the system both environmentally and socially balanced.

Germany is also known for pioneering feed-in tariffs (FiTs) under its Renewable Energy Sources Act (EEG). FiTs guarantee renewable energy producers—solar, wind, biogas, hydro—a fixed price for the electricity they feed into the grid, ensuring long-term investment security. This MBI triggered one of the world's fastest renewable energy booms and positioned Germany as a global leader in solar and wind deployment. More recently, competitive renewable energy auctions have replaced FiTs to ensure cost efficiency while continuing to support clean energy expansion.

In waste management and circular economy, Germany employs an advanced suite of MBI. The Packaging Act mandates Extended Producer Responsibility (EPR), requiring producers to finance collection and recycling. The "Green Dot" system—one of Europe's earliest EPR models—encourages producers to minimize packaging waste through fee structures based on material type and recyclability. Deposit-refund systems for beverage containers further incentivize high recycling rates, achieving return rates above 95%. Landfill taxes and bans also shift waste toward recycling and recovery.

Water management incorporates economic instruments such as wastewater charges, incentivizing industries to reduce pollutant loads and adopt cleaner technologies. The fertilizer levy and nutrient-regulation pricing mechanisms aim to reduce nitrate pollution from agriculture. In biodiversity protection, conservation-offset markets require developers to compensate for ecological impacts by restoring equivalent habitats elsewhere.

Germany also uses MBIs to promote sustainable transport. Policies include vehicle registration taxes linked to CO_2 emissions, road tolls for heavy-duty vehicles based on pollution intensity, and incentives for electric vehicles such as purchase subsidies and tax exemptions.

Overall, Germany's comprehensive approach–combining carbon pricing, EPR schemes, renewable energy incentives, eco-taxes, and tradable permits–demonstrates how MBI can guide economic behaviour toward environmental sustainability. These instruments have played a crucial role in reducing emissions, improving recycling, and accelerating clean energy adoption, solidifying Germany's position as a global leader in green market governance.

Eco-taxation has emerged as a core market-based instrument across OECD countries to address climate change, pollution, and resource degradation. These taxes–covering carbon, energy, transport, pollution, and waste–are designed to internalize environmental externalities and align economic incentives with sustainability goals. OECD experience shows that eco-taxes work best when combined with clear price signals, predictable tax trajectories, and complementary regulatory frameworks. Their effectiveness has been demonstrated in several contexts, yet important limitations persist, especially regarding equity, competitiveness, and political acceptance.

OECD countries have been pioneer in carbon pricing, fuel taxes, landfill charges, water pricing, and product taxes. In nations such as Sweden, Denmark, Finland, Germany, the UK, and the Netherlands, these instruments have significantly reduced pollution and shifted consumption patterns. For example, Nordic countries' early adoption of carbon taxes helped cut CO_2 emissions while maintaining economic growth, demonstrating that environmental taxes can decouple emissions from GDP. Energy taxes in Germany and the UK have promoted energy efficiency, reduced fossil fuel use, and stimulated investments in cleaner technologies. Transport-related eco-taxes–such as CO_2-linked vehicle registration fees, congestion pricing (London, Stockholm), and aviation taxes–have reduced urban emissions and promoted public transport. Waste and product taxes, including Pay As You Throw (PAYT) systems and levies on plastics and harmful chemicals, have contributed to circular-economy transitions. Similarly, landfill taxes in the UK, Denmark, and Sweden have drastically reduced landfill disposal and expanded recycling–showing strong behavioural impacts when substitutes exist. Thus, one clear strength of environmental taxes in OECD nations is their proven capacity to internalize environmental costs and send strong price signals. However, their success depends heavily on tax design. Taxes work best when rates are high, predictable, and broad-based. In reality, many OECD countries keep rates below socially optimal levels due to political pressures and lobbying from energy-intensive industries. Exemptions for aviation fuel, agriculture, or freight transport weaken environmental incentives. Even where carbon taxes exist, coverage gaps and sectoral exclusions reduce overall effectiveness. As a result, emissions reductions are often lower than what climate science demands.

Another limitation is its regressive impacts. Energy and carbon taxes can disproportionately affect low-income households because a higher share of their income goes toward energy consumption. OECD experience shows that poorly designed taxes without compensation measures—such as France's carbon tax protests ("Gilets Jaunes")—can provoke strong social resistance. Countries like Sweden and Canada have addressed this through revenue recycling, returning tax proceeds via income-tax cuts or direct rebates. This highlights that environmental taxes are effective only when integrated with equity-focused redistribution policies.

Competitiveness concerns also affect political feasibility. Industries fear that higher energy or carbon costs will reduce competitiveness relative to countries with weaker regulations. OECD countries address this through transitional exemptions, free quotas (under the EU Emissions Trading System), or border carbon adjustment proposals. However, such measures dilute environmental incentives and slow the shift toward cleaner production.

A strength of OECD experience is that environmental taxes often generate substantial revenue—typically 2%–5% of total tax revenue—which is used to fund renewable energy, public transport, green infrastructure, and innovation. This "double dividend" improves environmental outcomes while enabling fiscal reforms. But critics argue that governments sometimes prioritize revenue stability over environmental ambition, thereby undermining long-term decarbonization goals.

Finally, environmental taxes perform best when they are part of a comprehensive policy mix. OECD studies show that combining taxes with standards, subsidies, innovation support, and information tools produces stronger outcomes than taxes alone. For example, the UK's landfill tax dramatically reduced landfill use, but only after being paired with recycling targets and infrastructure development.

Overall, OECD evidence confirms that eco-taxes are effective when designed with strong price signals, transparent revenue recycling, and integration with broader climate and energy policies. They offer important lessons for economies seeking to align fiscal policy with environmental sustainability. environmental taxes in OECD countries have been effective in reducing pollution and promoting cleaner technologies, but their full potential is often curtailed by political compromises, equity concerns, and sectoral exemptions. Robust design, transparent revenue recycling, and integration with broader climate policies are essential for maximizing efficacy.

Chapter 5:

Eco Tax In India

Ancient Indian religious literature reflects a profound ecological consciousness, viewing nature not merely as a resource but as a sacred, living entity. The Vedas, particularly the Atharva Veda, emphasize harmony between humans and the environment. The Prithvi Sukta declares: "Earth is my mother, I am her son", underscoring an ethic of care and reciprocity. Natural elements such as air, water, fire, forests, and rivers were deified, promoting reverence and restraint in their use. The Upanishads advanced the idea of sustainable consumption. The Isha Upanishad states, "Tena tyaktena bhunjitha"–enjoy nature through renunciation, discouraging over-exploitation. The Vedas, Upanishads, Puranas and Smriti contain the earliest messages for preservation of environment and ecological balance. Nature, or Earth, has been engrained as a part of existence of life. The elements of nature have never been considered as hostile to be conquered or dominated but in fact possessing their own personalities. In the ancient Indian philosophy, it is forbidden to exploit nature for vilaas or luxury. To live in harmony with nature and recognize that divinity prevails in all elements, including plants and animals is the core philosophy. The saints, ascetics lived in the deepest of forests and mountains to be one with the eternal truth thus signifying that the existential questions are best understood within the cradle of a natural environment. Ecology is an inherent part of a spiritual worldview in Hinduism. Protection and preservation of environment is rooted in our culture heritage. Early regulatory frameworks are evident in the Smritis, which prescribed penalties for cutting trees and polluting water bodies. Yajnavalkya Smriti, a historic Indian text on statecraft and jurisprudence written before the 5th century AD, prohibited the cutting of trees and prescribed punishment for such acts. The epics, Ramayana and Mahabharata, portray forests (aranyas) as spaces of learning and spiritual growth and condemn the destruction of flora and fauna, linking environmental protection with dharma. The Arthashastra of Kautilya provides a systematic account of State-led conservation, including forest classification, wildlife protection, and water management, administered by officials like the Vanadhyaksha.

Buddhist and Jain texts, through the doctrine of *ahimsa*, extended moral consideration to all living beings. Kautalya's Arthashastra, written in Mauryan period, emphasised the need for forest administration. Ashoka went further, and his seventh Pillar Edicts expressed his view about the welfare of environment and biodiversity. It expresses that "Happiness in this world and the next is difficult to obtain without much love for the dhamma, much self-examination, much respect, much fear of evil, and much enthusiasm. [...] Beloved-of-the-Gods, King Piyadasi (Ashoka), speaks thus: Animals were declared to be protected - parrots, mainas, aruna, geese, wild ducks, nandimukhas, gelatas, bats, queen ants, terrapins, boneless fish, vedareyaka, gangapuputaka, sankiya fish, tortoises, porcupines, squirrels, deer, bulls, okapinda, wild asses, wild pigeons, domestic pigeons and all four-footed creatures that are neither useful nor edible. Thus, ancient Indian texts articulated principles of sustainability, restraint, and intergenerational equity, forming the ethical foundation of India's modern environmental jurisprudence reflected in Articles 48A and 51A(g) of the Constitution.

Since Independence, India's developmental trajectory has placed immense pressure on its environment, leading to significant ecological degradation and biodiversity loss. Rapid industrialization, urbanization, population growth, and infrastructure expansion have altered natural ecosystems at an unprecedented scale. Large-scale deforestation for agriculture, dams, mining, and urban expansion has resulted in the fragmentation of forests and loss of wildlife habitats, particularly in biodiversity-rich regions such as the Western Ghats, Central India, and the North-East. The Green Revolution, while ensuring food security, intensified the use of chemical fertilizers, pesticides, and groundwater extraction, causing soil degradation, water pollution, and loss of agro-biodiversity. Wetlands, mangroves, and coastal ecosystems have declined sharply due to land reclamation, port development, aquaculture, and pollution, increasing vulnerability to floods and cyclones. River systems have been severely affected by dam construction, sand mining, and industrial effluents, disrupting aquatic biodiversity. India has also witnessed a steady decline in species diversity, with several plants and animals becoming endangered due to habitat loss, poaching, invasive species, and climate change. Urban air and water pollution have further degraded ecosystems and human health. Climate change has intensified these stresses, evident in rising temperatures, erratic monsoons, glacier retreat, and increased frequency of extreme weather events. In the latest (2024) Yale Environmental Performance Index (EPI), India ranks near the bottom among evaluated countries (176th out of about 180 nations). The EPI assesses countries on indicators related to environmental health and ecosystem vitality, including air quality, climate change mitigation, biodiversity, and waste management. India's low ranking is primarily attributed to poor air quality, high greenhouse gas emissions intensity, pressure on natural ecosystems, and inadequate waste management, despite progress in renewable energy and climate commitments. The ranking highlights the gap between policy intent and on-ground environmental outcomes. The World Bank has highlighted that environmental degradation imposes a heavy economic cost on India, estimated at around USD 80 billion annually, underscoring the close linkage between environmental quality and economic development. This estimate, drawn from World Bank assessments on the Cost of Environmental Degradation (COED), represents a significant share of India's GDP and reflects losses arising from pollution, resource depletion, and ecosystem damage. A major component of this cost comes from air pollution, particularly ambient and household air pollution. High levels of particulate matter ($PM_{2.5}$) in urban and rural areas contribute to premature deaths, respiratory illnesses, reduced labour productivity, and increased healthcare expenditure. The World Bank has consistently identified air pollution as the single largest environmental health risk in India, with economic losses stemming from morbidity, mortality, and lost workdays. The World Bank emphasizes that environmental degradation is not merely an ecological issue but a development and poverty challenge, disproportionately affecting the poor and vulnerable. It recommends stronger environmental regulation, market-based instruments such as pollution pricing, investments in clean energy and urban infrastructure, and better integration of environmental concerns into economic planning. Overall, the estimate of USD 80 billion annually serves as a stark reminder that neglecting the environment carries substantial economic costs, and that sustainable environmental management is essential for India's long-term growth and human well-being.

Recognizing these challenges, India has enacted laws such as the Wildlife Protection Act, 1972, Forest Conservation Act, 1980, and Environment Protection Act, 1986, and expanded protected areas. However, enforcement gaps and development–environment trade-offs persist. The post-independence experience thus highlights the urgent need for sustainable development, ecological restoration, and community-based conservation to arrest further environmental loss. Our Environmental policy in India is traditionally rooted in command-and-control regime. The policy pursued by the authorities to meet environmental challenges posed by air, water, and solid waste pollution is mainly command-and-control in nature. The environmental laws enacted in India such as The Wildlife (Protection) Act 1972, Forests (Conservation) Act 1980, The Water

(Prevention and Control of Pollution) Act 1974 and The Air (Prevention and Control of Pollution) Act 1981 as well as the various Rules emanating from them are in the nature of 'command-and-control` regulation. While there may not be much scope for market based instruments (MBI) in the case of wild life protection, there is certainly good scope for employing market instruments for controlling water effluents, air pollution and waste disposal. Although, most of these regulations are, in the nature of 'command and control` (CAC), Governments also have a range of environmental policy tools at their disposal, which are market-based instruments (such as taxes and tradable permits), negotiated agreements, subsidies, environmental management systems and information campaigns. Although no single instrument can be considered best to address every environmental challenge, there has been a growing movement towards environmentally related taxation (and tradable permits) in various economies. After the 1992 Rio conference, employing MBI to promote environmental objectives have become increasingly popular. The term MBI covers a wide range of instruments including eco taxes. As we have just discussed in previous chapter, advanced economies of the West have been moving increasingly towards market-based approaches to environmental control. These new approaches allow individuals or companies greater flexibility in deciding where, when, how or to what extent to cut pollution emissions, thereby reducing the cost to the economy and increasing personal freedom. If properly designed, market-based systems allow reductions of pollution emissions with greater flexibility and with lower cost than with less flexible and comprehensive approaches. International experience has demonstrated that eco taxes can be very effective in their environmental impact. In a study by Sterner (2007) has concluded that "had Europe not followed a policy of high fuel taxation then fuel demand would have been twice as large". Sterner argues that high fuel taxation in Europe significantly curtailed fuel demand. His finding that fuel consumption would have been twice as large in the absence of high fuel taxes highlights the strong price elasticity of fuel demand in the long run. While short-term fuel demand tends to be inelastic, sustained high prices encourage structural changes such adoption of fuel-efficient vehicles, shift towards public transport, compact urban planning, reduced vehicle kilometers travelled, etc. Thus, fuel taxes worked not merely as a revenue tool but as a behavioural and technological driver, discouraging excessive fossil fuel use and associated emissions. Many European countries used fuel tax revenues to finance public transport, renewable energy, and social welfare, enhancing political acceptability. Sterner's conclusion holds important lessons for India, where fuel taxes are often driven by fiscal considerations rather than environmental objectives. A predictable, environment-linked fuel taxation framework, combined with investment in public transport and clean mobility, could reduce oil dependence and emissions while supporting sustainable development.

The study of environmental regulation in developed countries, clearly shows that they are increasingly resorting to MBI like eco taxes to protect environment. They are doing so in conjunction with Command- and-control (CAC) approach or in preference to CAC approach. India may also take lessons from experiences of these countries for environmental regulation. India is also facing severe environmental pressure in pursuance of its development agenda. Increasing population growth and urbanization has radically impacted the ecology. Charging the full social cost of pollution gives firms and individuals the incentive to pollute less when the cost of pollution abatement is less than the social cost of pollution. One way of internalizing external costs is through eco taxes. Such taxes cause polluters or resource users to pay for the environmental resources they use, just as they pay for capital and labour. Environmental taxation has a significant role to play in addressing environmental challenges. Taxes can be extremely effective when they are properly designed, are levied as close to the environmentally damaging pollutant or activity as possible, and are set at an adequate rate. The revenues generated can be used to help with fiscal consolidation or reduce other tax rates. Environmental taxes give rise to distributional or competitiveness concerns, but these are usually best addressed through other policies tools. Providing information, transparency, and certainty are critical to public acceptance and to the effectiveness of environmental taxation. Finally, taxes may need to be combined with other instruments to obtain the most efficient and effective environmental policy package, but care should be taken to assess the impact of overlapping instruments. Tax differentiation involves a positive charge being levied on a polluting product and a negative charge, or subsidy, on a cleaner alternative. The most common example of this tax differential is in the context of transport to discourage purchases of polluting vehicles or fuels. Less tax on compressed natural gas (CNG) vis-à-vis petrol in Delhi is one such example. By making dirty fuels like oil and coal more expensive, a carbon tax encourages utilities, businesses and individuals to reduce energy consumption and increase energy efficiency. A carbon tax also makes clean, renewable energy from sources such as wind and solar more cost-competitive with fossil fuels.

Eco tax has many advantages, such as environmental effectiveness, economic efficiency, the ability to raise public revenue, and transparency. Also, eco taxes have been successfully used to address a wide range of issues including waste disposal, water pollution and air emissions. Regardless of the policy area, the design of eco taxes and political economy considerations in their implementation are crucial determinants of their overall success. In 2007, the Madras School of Economics (MSE) under the guidance of Prof. Raja Chelliah had suggested for introduction of grade wise 'cess on coal' differentiated by the ash content in coal. The following grade wise rates on cess on coal were recommended by MSE:

Grade/Type of Coal			Rate (Per tonne)
(A)	Coking Coal		
	(i)	All varieties of coking coal where ash content is 18% or less	Nil
	(ii)	All varieties of coking coal where ash content is between 19% to 28%	₹ 20
	(iii)	All varieties of coking coal where ash content is more than 28% or	₹ 40
(B)	Non-Coking Coal		
	(i)	All varieties of coking coal where ash content is less than 28%	Nil
	(ii)	All varieties of coking coal where ash content is higher than 28%	₹ 50

Through Finance Bill 2010-11 a corpus called National Clean Energy Fund (NCEF) was created out of cess on coal produced / imported ("polluter pays" principle) for the purposes of financing and promoting clean energy initiatives and funding research in the area of clean energy. However, this was not in line with MSE's proposal recommending imposition of grade wise cess on coal. Details of its notification by Government of India may be seen at Annex:1. In the Indian taxation system, a cess is a fee levied to raise funds for a specific purpose (Comptroller and Auditor General of India, 2017). The coal cess is levied on the dispatch of coal and lignite by coal producers and discourages coal consumption by increasing its cost. In this case, the purpose was to mobilize funds for supporting renewable energy through the NCEF. The policy design was to earmark part of the revenues from the coal cess for the NCEF that, in turn, funded research and innovative projects in clean energy. Since its inception, the coal cess has been increased eight times, from ₹50 per tonne in 2010 to ₹200 per tonne in March 2015 and ₹400 per tonne in March 2016 (Garg et al., 2017). With the introduction of the Goods and Service Tax (GST) in India in July 2017, the Clean Energy Cess was abolished by the Taxation Laws Amendment Act, 2017. A new cess on coal production, called the

GST Compensation Cess, was put in its place at the same rate of ₹400 per tonne. The GST Compensation Cess is aimed at filling in the budget deficits that Indian states faced following the GST introduction. Until recently, coal had a 5% GST rate plus a flat ₹400 per tonne compensation cess, regardless of the coal's quality or price. From September 2025 onwards, the GST rate is 18%, and the flat cess has been removed.

Over FY 2010–2018, India collected ₹86,440 crore (almost USD 12 billion) worth of the coal cess (Department of Expenditure, 2018). The fund, managed under Department of Expenditure under Ministry of Finance, serves as a non-lapsable corpus to promote research, innovation, and deployment of renewable technologies. NCEF finances initiatives like solar, wind, tidal and geothermal energy projects, smart grids, and community energy solutions, while aiding National Action Plan on Climate Change missions. It targets reducing carbon intensity and emissions in line with India's 2009 commitments. However, as a low-middle-income country, India has many competing development needs, and not all revenue from the coal cess went to support renewable through the NCEF. In 2017, large-scale and solar renewable energy reached grid parity costs in India, meaning that these were competitive without subsidies. Meanwhile, the GST reform caused large budget deficits at the State level (Garg et al., 2017). This situation made Indian policy-makers re-prioritize the use of revenues from taxation of coal production despite the fact that many renewable energy technologies, especially small-scale energy access solutions such as distributed solar or clean cooking stoves, need financial support from the government and could be funded from the NCEF.

An Inter- Ministerial Group (IMG) chaired by Finance Secretary approves the projects/schemes eligible for financing under the NCEF. These projects include innovative schemes like Green Energy Corridor for boosting up the transmission sector, Namami Gange, Green India Mission, Jawaharlal Nehru National Solar Mission

(JNNSM)'s installation of solar photovoltaic (SPV) lights and small capacity lights, installation of SPV water pumping systems, SPV power plants, Grid Connected Rooftop SPV Power Plants, pilot project to assess wind power potential etc.

Between 2010-11 to 2017-18, IMG has recommended 55 projects of ₹34811.19 crore. For 2017-18, ₹8703 crore have been provided for in the Budget for NCEF projects. The coal cess was collected at ₹50.00 per tonne of coal since June22, 2010 which was extended in Budget 2014-15 to ₹100.00 per tonne of coal w.e.f. 11.07.2014. The same was increased to ₹200.00 per tonne w.e.f. 01.03.2015 in the 2015-16 Budget. Further, the coal cess has been increased to ₹400 per tonne in the Union budget 2016-17 and the same has been renamed as "Clean Environment Cess". Accordingly, the name of NCEF has been changed to National Clean Energy and Environment Fund (NCEEF).

However, the Goods and Services Tax (Compensation to States) Act, 2017 which has been notified on 12.04.2017, provides that coal cess, along with some other cess on pan masala, tobacco, aerated water etc. would constitute GST Compensation Fund and the same would be utilized to compensate the States for five years to compensate them for potential losses on account of GST implementation. After five years any amount left would be shared on 50% basis between Centre and States. Details of fund position over the years in NCEEF are at Annex: 2. NCEF today is largely a legacy/defunct mechanism, with its role absorbed into general budgetary and climate finance frameworks. Clean energy spending now financed through budgetary support to MNRE, viability gap funding schemes, and Other climate finance instrument.

In the end, National Clean Energy Fund (NCEF)/National Clean Energy and Environment Fund (NCEEF) was established by the Government of India in 2010–11 to finance and promote clean energy initiatives and technologies. It was created by levying a clean energy cess on coal produced and imported in India, based on the "polluter pays" principle. The primary objective of the Fund was to support research, innovation, and deployment of clean energy projects, including renewable energy, energy efficiency, and low-carbon technologies. Funds were routed through ministries such as MNRE, MoEFCC, and were also used for projects like National Carbon Market readiness and green infrastructure. However, over time, a significant portion of NCEF was diverted for non-clean energy purposes, including compensating States for GST revenue loss, diluting its original intent. With the introduction of the GST in 2017, the coal cess was subsumed into the GST Compensation Cess, and NCEF gradually lost relevance. Despite its limitations, NCEF/NCEEF marked India's first major fiscal instrument dedicated to clean energy financing.

Water Cess

The Water (Prevention and Control of Pollution) Act was enacted in 1974 to provide for the prevention and control of water pollution, and for maintaining or restoring of wholesomeness of water in the country. The Water (Prevention and Control of Pollution) Cess Act was enacted in 1977, and it is levied on industries and local authorities for the consumption of water, with the objective of augmenting the financial resources of the Central and State Pollution Control Boards. It was established under the Water (Prevention and Control of Pollution) Cess Act, 1977, which was enacted by the Government of India to support the effective implementation of the Water (Prevention and Control of Pollution) Act, 1974. The cess aimed to promote efficient water use, reduce wastage, and control water pollution by creating economic disincentives for excessive water consumption by industries and municipalities. This cess is collected with a view to augment the resources of the Central Pollution Control Board and the State Pollution Control Boards for the prevention and control of water pollution constituted under the Water (Prevention and Control of Pollution) Act, 1974. The Act was last amended in 2003. The cess was applied by local authorities (such as municipalities responsible for supplying water for domestic and industrial use) to industries involved in manufacturing, processing, and operations using water for specific purposes. Categories of industries covered under the Act included: fertilisers, paper, steel, textiles, chemicals, cement, food processing industries, thermal power plants and other water-intensive sectors. The cess was levied based on the quantity of water consumed by industries and local authorities, measured through installed water meters.

The purposes for which water consumption was chargeable included industrial cooling or boiler feed, domestic purposes, processing that resulted in water pollution. Levied rates varied depending on the category of industry, use of water, and extent of pollution generated. The rates were expressed in paisa per kilolitre of water consumed. To encourage compliance and pollution control, the Act provided for a rebate to industries that adopted approved measures for the treatment, reuse, and recycling of wastewater. Initially, industries could claim a 25% rebate on the cess amount if they installed and operated effluent treatment plants (ETPs). The rebate served as an incentive for industries to invest in pollution control infrastructure and adopt sustainable practices. The cess collected was credited to the Consolidated Fund of India, and a portion of it was disbursed to the Central and State Pollution Control Boards. The funds were utilised for: monitoring and controlling water pollution, strengthening laboratory and monitoring infrastructure, conducting water quality assessments and supporting research, training, and public awareness on pollution control.

Central Government was responsible for levying and collecting the cess, and framing rules. Central Pollution Control Board received funds from Central Government to coordinate national-level water pollution control efforts. State Pollution Control Boards (SPCBs) implemented the Act at the State level and ensured compliance by industries. Local Authorities reported water consumption data and assisted in cess collection. The Water (Prevention and Control of Pollution) Cess Act, 1977 was repealed through the Taxation Laws (Amendment) Act, 2017, and the cess mechanism was withdrawn. Following this, the collection of cess was discontinued, and alternative mechanisms for funding the Pollution Control Boards were introduced. The repeal aimed to simplify the tax structure and eliminate redundant levies in line with the Goods and Services Tax (GST) regime. Now, the Pollution Control Boards are financed through budgetary allocations from the Central and State Governments, consent fees from industries, and other sources. Despite its repeal, the Water Pollution Cess played a significant role in India's early environmental policy framework. It generated financial resources for pollution control institutions, created economic incentives for industries to adopt cleaner technologies, encouraged the practice of measuring and metering water consumption and raised awareness about the cost of water pollution and sustainable resource use.

The Water (Prevention and Control of Pollution) Cess mechanism represented an early effort to integrate economic instruments into environmental management in India. It established the principle of "polluter pays", where users of natural resources bear the cost of preventing and mitigating pollution. Although repealed, its legacy continues in India's approach to environmental regulation, influencing the design of modern environmental taxes, fees, and incentive-based pollution control mechanisms. The Water (Prevention and Control of Pollution) Cess Act, 1977 was a pioneering initiative in India's environmental policy, aimed at conserving water resources and funding pollution control efforts. By linking water usage with financial responsibility, it encouraged industries to adopt efficient and sustainable practices.

States with green tax on vehicles

Several States in India have implemented green taxes on vehicles to curb pollution from older, higher-emission models. The tax is often a percentage of the road tax and is collected at the time of fitness or registration renewal. Some States also charge a green cess on vehicles entering from other States. Green tax is a financial levy imposed by governments on sources (for example vehicle) that contribute to environmental pollution, particularly air pollution from vehicular emissions. The tax serves both as a deterrent to excessive polluting vehicle use and as a revenue source for ecological initiatives. Several Indian States currently levy eco tax (green tax) to curb vehicular pollution, primarily targeting older vehicles and out-of State- entries. Most of these States charge green tax on commercial vehicles older than 8 years and private vehicles older than 15 years often with exemptions for local, electric, CNG, Government, or emergency vehicles. The collected revenue is typically dedicated to pollution control, improving air quality and sustainable urban transport initiatives.

Andhra Pradesh levies a green tax on older transport and non-transport vehicles. Delhi imposes an Environmental Compensation Charge (ECC) on commercial vehicles entering the city. Goa charges a 0.5% green cess on petrol and diesel. Himachal Pradesh imposes similar green levy on vehicles from other States entering tourist areas. Jharkhand imposes green taxes primarily on older vehicles. Karnataka charges green taxes on older vehicles. Kerala imposes a green tax on vehicles over 15 years old. Madhya Pradesh charges green taxes, mainly on older vehicles. Maharashtra levies green taxes ranging from ₹200 to ₹10,000, depending on the vehicle's age and type. Meghalaya has a pollution surcharge on petrol and diesel. Punjab imposes a cess and special infrastructure development fee on petrol and diesel. Rajasthan levies green taxes, predominantly on older vehicles. Tamil Nadu applies a green tax on vehicles older than 15 years. Telangana levies green taxes, primarily on older vehicles.

West Bengal has a cess included in its sales tax for petrol and diesel. Uttarakhand government will begin collecting a tax from vehicles entering the State from other States starting December 2025. The decision of the State Government aims to control vehicular pollution, protect the fragile Himalayan ecosystem, and promote environmental cleanliness across the State. The automated tax collection system will use Automatic Number Plate Recognition (ANPR) cameras installed at the State's entry points to capture the registration numbers of incoming vehicles. The captured data will be transmitted to the National Payments Corporation of India (NPCI) database, where, after verification, the applicable tax amount will be automatically deducted from the vehicle owner's payment wallet and credited to the transport department's account. However, exemption would be made in case of those vehicles registered in Uttarakhand, electric and CNG vehicles, ambulances, fire brigade trucks, and two-wheelers will be exempt from the green tax, while vehicles re-entering the State within 24 hours will also not be charged again.

States Levying Eco or Green Taxes (as of 2025)

State / UT	**Type of Eco/Green Tax**	**Applicable Rate / Rule**	**Status**
Maharashtra	Green tax on vehicles	₹200–₹1,000 for two-wheelers, ₹500–₹3,000 for four-wheelers; collected at fitness renewal	Active
Delhi (NCT)	Environmental compensation on old diesel/petrol vehicles; ECC on trucks entering Delhi	₹700–₹1,300 per truck; 10-year diesel ban	Active
Karnataka	Green tax on vehicles over 15 years old	₹250 (two-wheelers) – ₹1,500 (four-wheelers)	Active
Tamil Nadu	Green tax at vehicle re-registration (15 years old)	₹250–₹1,000	Active

Kerala	Green tax on old vehicles	₹200–₹2,000 at re-registration	Active
Haryana	ECC on commercial vehicles entering NCR area	₹700–₹1,300	Active
Himachal Pradesh	Green fee on tourist vehicles entering State	₹100–₹500	Active
Goa	Green cess on hotel stays, mining, and industries	0.25%–1% on turnover (varies)	Active
Rajasthan	Green tax on vehicles older than 15 years	₹250–₹1,000	Active
Uttarakhand	Entry tax on tourist vehicles for eco zones	₹50–₹250	Active
Madhya Pradesh	Green tax on vehicles over 15 years	₹250–₹1,500	Active
Gujarat	Green cess on industries (proposed under GPCB)	In discussion stage	Proposed
Assam	Green tax on old vehicles	₹250–₹1,500	Active
Sikkim	Eco fee on tourists entering protected zones	₹100–₹500	Active
Nagaland	Eco fees on tourists at specific checkpoints	₹50–₹200	Limited scope

Source: State Governments

The Green Tax aims to encourage car owners to replace their outdated vehicles with newer, greener models that leave fewer environmental footprints. This strategy encourages the use of greener technologies while also assisting in the reduction of pollution. Beyond merely being a tax, the Green Tax serves as a behavioral incentive, pushing people to look into more environmentally friendly modes of transportation. These include electric scooters, which are gaining popularity as people become more aware of their carbon footprint. This project is essential in preventing global warming and promoting environmental sustainability since it is directing the transition to more environmentally friendly automobiles. In India, the Green Tax is applicable when a vehicle's registration is renewed, especially for older cars. This tax applies to individual automobiles over fifteen years old and commercial vehicles over eight years old. The emphasis is on reducing the increased pollution levels brought on by antiquated engines in older cars.

Green Tax on Older Vehicles

The Union Minister for Road Transport and Highways, Shri Nitin Gadkari has approved a proposal to levy a "Green Tax" on old vehicles which are polluting the environment in 2021. The proposal was sent to the States for consultation before it is formally notified. The main principles to be followed while levying the Green Tax are:

- Transport vehicles older than 8 years could be charged Green Tax at the time of renewal of fitness certificate, at the rate of 10 to 25 % of road tax;
- Personal vehicles to be charged Green Tax at the time of renewal of Registration Certification after 15 years;
- Public transport vehicles, such as city buses, to be charged lower Green tax;
- Higher Green tax (50% of Road Tax) for vehicles being registered in highly polluted cities
- Differential tax, depending on fuel (petrol/diesel) and type of vehicle;
- Vehicles like strong hybrids, electric vehicles and alternate fuels like CNG, ethanol, LPG, etc. to be exempted;
- Vehicles used in farming, such as tractor, harvester, tiller, etc. to be exempted;
- Revenue collected from the Green Tax to be kept in a separate account and used for tackling pollution, and for States to set up state-of-art facilities for emission monitoring

The benefits of the "Green Tax" could be:

- To dissuade people from using vehicles which damage the environment
- To motivate people to switch to newer, less polluting vehicles
- Green tax will reduce the pollution level, and make the polluter pay for pollution.

The Minister also approved the policy of deregistration and scrapping of vehicles owned by Government department and PSU, which are above 15 years in age. It is estimated that commercial vehicles, which constitute about 5% of the total vehicle fleet, contribute about 65%-70% of total vehicular pollution. The older fleet, typically manufactured before the year 2000 constitute less than 1 % of the total fleet but contributes around 15% of total vehicular pollution. These older vehicles pollute 10-25 times more than modern vehicles.

States with eco-taxes on Mining

Following a Supreme Court ruling in August 2024, States gained the power to levy taxes on mineral-bearing land and mineral rights retrospectively from April 2005. In this regard, Karnataka has recently passed a bill in December 2024 to impose new taxes on mineral rights, with the Central government evaluating legal strategies to mitigate its impact. Odisha, Tamil Nadu, Rajasthan, Chhattisgarh and Uttar Pradesh have also raised tax demands following the Supreme Court's ruling.

Plastic pollution problem

Plastic pollution has emerged as one of the most severe environmental challenges facing India, affecting ecosystems, public health, urban governance, and economic sustainability. With rapid urbanization, population growth, changing consumption patterns, and the rise of single-use products, India generates an estimated 3.5–

4 million tonnes of plastic waste annually, of which a significant proportion is mismanaged.

A major problem lies in the dominance of single-use plastics such as carry bags, food packaging, bottles, straws, and disposable cutlery. These items have a short lifespan but persist in the environment for hundreds of years. Despite bans and regulations, weak enforcement, low public awareness, and availability of cheap alternatives continue to fuel their widespread use. Inadequate waste management infrastructure further aggravates the issue. Segregation of waste at source remains poor, and urban local bodies are often overburdened. As a result, large quantities of plastic waste end up in open dumps, landfills, drains, rivers, and coastal areas. Plastic clogging urban drainage systems contributes to urban flooding, particularly during monsoons, as witnessed in cities like Mumbai, Chennai, and Bengaluru.

Plastic pollution has severe ecological impacts. Terrestrial and aquatic animals ingest plastic debris, mistaking it for food, leading to injury or death. India's rivers, especially the Ganga, Yamuna, and Indus system, transport plastic waste to the oceans, contributing significantly to marine plastic pollution. Micro plastics formed by the breakdown of larger plastics have entered soil, water, and the food chain, posing long-term risks to biodiversity and human health.

The informal recycling sector, while crucial for plastic recovery, operates under unsafe conditions with limited technological capacity, leading to low-quality recycling and environmental hazards. Moreover, multi-layered plastics used in food packaging are difficult to recycle and often end up being burned, releasing toxic pollutants such as dioxins and furans.

Recognizing the scale of the problem, India has introduced measures like the Plastic Waste Management Rules, Extended Producer Responsibility (EPR), and a nationwide ban on selected single-use plastic items from July 2022. However, persistent challenges highlight the need for behavioural change, effective enforcement, alternative materials, improved recycling technologies, and circular economy approaches. Addressing plastic pollution is essential for achieving sustainable development, environmental protection, and public health security in India.

Plastics and the GST reform

One of India's biggest tax reforms in recent history was the introduction of the Goods and Services Tax (GST) in July 2017. Prior to this, plastic was taxed at the national level via 12.5% manufacturing duty and 5% VAT. In the new GST regime, plastic products are taxed at 18%. Although this didn't substantially increase the cost of plastics, it did create further confusion due to the different types of plastic used in a wide range of products and the various rates and exemptions that might apply for different categories of goods, as well as the successive modification of GST rates. Initial evidence points to the GST reform having an adverse impact on plastic recycling, as during the first four months of implementation, it discouraged traders from buying recyclable plastic from rag pickers and scrap-sellers. As a result, the GST Council drastically reduced the rate from 18% to 5% on plastic and other waste in October 2017.

Taxing plastic production

Plastic tax reforms in most countries have concentrated on taxing at the consumption level (like taxing plastic bags in supermarkets), taxes can also be targeted at the manufacturing level, for example on virgin materials as opposed to recycled materials in the production process. The British Treasury levied a new tax on the manufacture and import of plastic packaging that contains less than 30% recycled content. A tax of this kind would lead to several positive outcomes: increasing resource efficiency by reducing the use of virgin plastics and increasing the use of recycled plastics in production, which would create greater demand for recycled plastic upstream in the supply chain, and in turn expand incentives for increased collection and recycling of plastic material downstream. As such, this tax is a good example of a policy that facilitates transition from the linear economy (make, use, dispose, pollute) to the circular economy, where the maximum value is extracted from resources whilst in use, and then materials are reused, remade and recycled to their full potential in order to minimise waste.

In order to tackle its plastic waste crisis, India should design a similar tax to the UK's, which complements the existing GST regime. Although tax revenues are not generally earmarked for specific purposes, revenues from this tax could be allocated to enhancing plastic collection and recycling infrastructure, and improving the working conditions of rag pickers. In order to move forward with the design and implementation of a plastics production tax in India, the next steps should be to examine existing economic incentives and disincentives for plastic production, consumption and recycling, and evaluating how various tax design options would influence them. Apart from this, building alliances with stakeholders from the taxation, environmental and waste management communities to ensure the design of the tax is appropriate and increase the likelihood of its effective and successful implementation.

India does not follow a single, comprehensive eco-tax regime; instead, it applies a range of sector-specific environmental levies. One of the earliest examples is the cess on coal, introduced in 2010 as the Clean Energy cess and it aims to discourage excessive coal consumption and generate funds for clean energy and environmental initiatives. Similarly, carbon-related taxes on petrol and diesel, levied through excise duties, indirectly function as eco-taxes by pricing fossil fuel use and influencing consumer behaviour.

At the local level, several municipalities impose green taxes on old vehicles, particularly diesel vehicles entering urban areas, to reduce air pollution. States such as Himachal Pradesh and Uttarakhand levy environmental or green taxes on tourists vehicles to mitigate ecological stress in fragile hill ecosystems. In addition, plastic waste management fees and charges on single-use plastics reflect the eco-tax principle of "polluter pays."

However, eco taxation in India faces challenges such as concerns over inflationary impacts, regressivity affecting poorer households, fragmented implementation, and limited earmarking of revenues for environmental purposes. Their effectiveness is also constrained by challenges such as low tax rates, weak earmarking of revenues for environmental purposes, and political resistance due to inflationary concerns. To enhance effectiveness, India needs a more coherent eco tax policy, better use of revenues for green investments, and integration with broader environmental and climate strategies.

Overall, eco taxes in India represent a promising pathway to reconcile economic growth with environmental preservation by embedding sustainability within fiscal policy. Eco-taxes in India serve multiple objectives: they discourage environmentally harmful activities, mobilize resources for conservation, and promote cleaner technologies. Eco-taxes have significant potential and strengthening their design through clear environmental objectives, transparent use of revenues, and integration with market-based instruments like emissions trading schemes can enhance their impact. In the context of climate change, pollution, and resource depletion, eco-taxes can play a vital role in steering India towards environmentally sustainable and economically efficient growth.

Annex: 1

F.No.354/72/2010-TRU
Government of India
Ministry of Finance
Department of Revenue
(Tax Research Unit)

New Delhi, 24.06.10

To

Chief Commissioners of Central Excise (All),
Chief Commissioners of Customs (All),
Chief Commissioners of Central Excise and Customs (All),
Director General of Central Excise Intelligence, New Delhi,
Director General of Audit, N. Delhi,
Director General of Revenue Intelligence, New Delhi.

Madam/Sir,

It may kindly be recalled that as part of the proposals contained in the Budget for 2010-11, Finance Minister had announced the imposition of Clean Energy Cess as a duty of excise on coal, lignite and peat. This cess is to come into force on a date to be notified by the Central Government after the enactment of the Finance Bill, 2010. In pursuance of the enactment of the Bill on 08.05.2010, it has been decided to notify 1st July, 2010 as the appointed date for coming into force of the provisions of Chapter VII (Section 83 and 84) of the Finance Act, 2010. Notification No.1/2010-CEC (Clean Energy Cess) dated 22.06.2010 has been issued for this purpose.

2. The Tenth Schedule to the Finance Act, 2010 prescribes a statutory rate of cess of ₹100 per tonne for all three categories, namely, coal, lignite and peat. An effective rate of ₹50 per tonne has

been prescribed through Notification No. 3/2010-CEC dated 22.06.2010. Notification No. 28/2010-CE and 29/2010-CE, both dated 22.06.2010 have also been issued to exempt such goods (i.e. to which the clean energy cess applies) from education cess and higher education cess respectively. As a result, the aggregate rate of cess would be ₹50 per tonne. This amount has to be paid in cash as suitable amendment in the CENVAT credit rules, 2004 is being made to exclude payment of this cess using credit.

3. The cess would apply to the gross quantity of raw coal, lignite or peat raised and dispatched from a coal mine. No deduction from this quantity is to be allowed for loss, if any, on account of washing of coal or its conversion into any other product/form prior to its dispatch from the mine. At the same time, cess would not be chargeable on washed coal or any other form provided the appropriate cess has been paid at the raw stage. In order to provide for this, all goods covered by the Tenth Schedule other than raw coal, raw lignite and peat are being exempted from the cess (Notification No.4/2010-CEC dated 22.06.2010) on the condition that appropriate cess has been paid at the raw stage.

4. Since Clean Energy Cess is being levied as a duty of excise, it would also apply to imported coal by virtue of Section 3(1) of the Customs Tariff Act in the form of additional duty of customs. As imported coal would not satisfy the condition regarding payment of appropriate cess at the raw stage, Clean Energy Cess would apply to all forms of imported coal including washed coal.

5. In the State of Meghalaya, coal is mined under traditional and customary rights vested on the local tribes. The mines operated by these tribes are not subjected to the provisions of laws that regulate the operation of coal mines. As such, full exemption from Clean Energy Cess is being provided to coal produced in the State of Meghalaya under such rights (Notification No. 5/2010-CEC dated 22.06.2010 refers).

6. Section 83 of the Finance Act, 2010 provides that the Central Government may by notification in the official gazette declare that any of the provisions of Central Excise Act, 1944 relating to levy, exemption, refund etc. would be applicable in respect of Clean energy Cess. In pursuance of this power, Notification No. 2/2010-Clean Energy Cess dated 22.06.2010 has been issued to borrow the relevant machinery provisions of the Central Excise Act, 1944 for the collection and administration of the cess.

7. Section 84 of the Finance Act, 2010 empowers the Central Government to make rules for carrying out the provisions of Chapter VII. Accordingly, Clean Energy Cess Rules, 2010 have been notified under this provision to prescribe a procedure for the levy and collection of the cess (Notification No. 6/2010- Clean Energy Cess dated 22.06.2010). These rules envisage simple compliance regime for coal mines akin to the one already in place in respect of stowing Excise Duty collected by the office of the Coal Controller, Government of India. The salient features of these rules are as under:

(i) Every producer of coal, lignite and peat is required to be registered with the jurisdictional central excise authority. This would imply that every coal mine should obtain registration. In several cases, especially in the case of coal mines operated by public sector undertakings such as Coal India Limited and its subsidiaries, the accounting and billing of coal is done in a centralised manner. In order to ease the compliance burden on such producers, an option has been given to obtain centralised registration for the office from where accounting or billing is done. With the introduction of ACES, the registration of Central Excise assesses is being undertaken exclusively in the electronic mode. Besides, the registration number generated electronically is required for making electronic payments of duty. In order to harmonise the processes in respect of Clean Energy Cess with Central Excise it has been decided that the application form for registration of Central Excise assesses would itself be used for the registration of assesses liable to pay Clean Energy Cess with the modification that the word "factory" would be read as "mine" in this case.

(ii) Cess would be payable on quantity removed during a month on self-assessment basis.

(iii) The due date for payment has been fixed as the 6th (for e-payment) / 5th (for payment in any other manner) of the month following the next month to which the removals relate i.e. payment for removals during the month of July, 2010 should be paid by the 5th/6th of September, 2010. However, on imports the cess would be payable w.e.f. 1st July, 2010.

(iv) Adjustment of excess payment, if any, is permissible by the next payment date.

(v) Monthly return indicating the total quantity removed along with cess payment has been prescribed. Since this return is not compatible with ACES software electronic filing would not be feasible at this stage. Returns may hence be accepted manually by the jurisdictional Range/Division of Central Excise.

(vi) General penalty of ₹10,000 has been prescribed for any contravention.

(vii) Specified goods are to be removed under cover of proper documents. However, this need not be an invoice. It has been prescribed in rule that any document specifying the quantity removed and name of the consignee would suffice.

8. Although the levy of Clean Energy Cess comes into force on the 1st of July, 2010, the first payment from registered producers would be due only by the 5th of September, 2010. In the meanwhile, the office of Chief Controller of Accounts has already been requested to assign a minor head for the payment of this cess both on domestic and imported coal. Relevant communication conveying this to the field formations would be issued in due course.

9. The provisions of the relevant notifications and this letter may be brought to the notice of field formations under your charge and the trade. The notifications may kindly be studied with utmost care and difficulties in their implementation, if any, may be brought to the notice of the undersigned.

Yours faithfully,

(Vivek Johri)
Joint Secretary (TRU-I)
Tel: 23092687

Annex:2

National Clean Energy Fund (NCEF) was established by the Government of India in 2010–11 to finance clean energy and environmental projects. It was primarily funded through a coal cess (Clean Environment Cess) levied on coal production and imports, based on the "polluter pays" principle. The objective of the fund was to support research, innovation, and deployment of clean energy technologies, including renewable energy, energy efficiency, and environmental protection initiatives. Over time, its scope expanded to include projects related to climate change mitigation and adaptation. The fund was administered by an inter-ministerial group, and various ministries could seek support for eligible projects. After the introduction of the Goods and Services Tax (GST) in 2017, the coal cess was replaced by the GST Compensation Cess, and the original structure of NCEF was subsumed under broader fiscal arrangements. Despite institutional changes, NCEF marked an important step in using fiscal instruments to promote sustainable development and low-carbon growth in India. Details of Fund Position over the years in NCEF/NCEEF are given below:

Year wise Details of project Recommended in NCEEF by the IMG

Year	Projects recommended by IMG to be financed from NCEEF (in ₹Crore)	No of Projects recommended by IMG
2010-2011	0.00	Nil
2011-2012	566.50	9
2012-2013	2715.11	6
2013-2014	1060.22	11

2014-15	12000.17	19
2015-16	18469.47	10
Total	34811.19	55

Source: Economic Survey 2016-17 and MoF brief.

Year	Coal Cess Collected (in ₹crores)	Amount transferred to NCEEF (in ₹crores)	Amounts financed from NCEEF for projects (in ₹crores)
2010-2011	1,066.46	0.00	0.00
2011-2012	2,579.55	1,066.46	220.75
2012-2013	3,053.19	1,500.00	246.43
2013-2014	3,471.98	1,650.00	1,218.78
2014-2015	5,393.46	4,700.00	2,087.99
2015-2016	12,675.60	5,123.09	5,234.80
2016-2017	28,500.00	6,902.74	6,902.74
2017-2018	29,700.00	8,703.00	-
Total	86,440.21	29,645.29	15,911.49

Source: Parliamentary Standing Committee on Renewable Energy

Ministry wise NCEEFF Fund allocation in different years (in ₹crores)

FY	MNRE	Ministry of Water Resources, River Development & Ganga Rejuvenation	Ministry of Drinking Water &Sanitation	Ministry of Environment & Forests	Ministry of Power	Ministry of Heavy Industries& Public Enterprises	Total
2010-	0	0	0	0	0	0	0

11							
2011-12	160.80	0	0	59.95	0	0	220.75
2012-13	125.78	0	110.65	10.00	0	0	246.43
2013-14	1,218.78	0	0	0	0	0	1,218.78
2014-15	1,977.35	0	110.64	0	0	0	2,087.99
2015-16	3,989.83	1,000.00	0	244.97	0	0	5,234.80
2016-17	4,272.00	1,675.00	0	955.74	0	0	6,902.74
2017-18	5,341.70	2,250.00	0	1,111.30	0	0	8,703.00
Total	17,086.24	4,925.00	221.29	2381.96	0	0	24,614.49

Source: Parliamentary Standing Committee on Renewable Energy

Ministry wise and Scheme-wise allocation of NCEEF funds for 2017-18

S. No.	Name of the Ministry/Scheme	Amount (in₹Cr.)
1	Ministry of Environment, Forest and Climate Change (MoEFCC)	
(i)	Climate Change Action Plan	40.00
(ii)	National Mission on Himalayan Studies	50.00
(iii)	National Adaptation Fund	110.00
(iv)	National Mission for Green India	157.30

(v)	Integrated Development of Wildlife Habitats	522.50
(vi)	Conservation of Natural resources and Ecosystems	91.00
(vii)	National River Conservation Programme	140.50
	Subtotal-Ministry of Environment, Forest and Climate Change	1,111.30
2	Ministry of New and Renewable Energy (MNRE)	
(i)	Grid Interactive Renewable Power	4034.50
(ii)	Off Grid/Distributed& Decentralized Renewable Power	918.20
(iii)	Research, Development and International co-operation	144.00
(iv)	Supporting Programmes	195.00
(v)	Other Central Sector Expenditure (PSUs)	50.00
	Subtotal-Ministry of New and Renewable Energy	5,341.70
3	Ministry of Water Resources, River Development and Ganga Rejuvenation	
(i)	NamamiGange: National Ganga Plan	2250.00
	Subtotal-Ministry of Water Resources, River Development and Ganga Rejuvenation	2250.00
	Total(1+2+3)	8,703.00

Source: Department of Expenditure, Ministry of Finance

References

Annual Report 2024-25, Ministry of Environment Forest and Climate Change

Annual Report 2021-22, Central Pollution Control Board

https://mnre.gov.in/en/annual-report-2024-25/

https://moef.gov.in/

https://mohua.gov.in/

https://cpcb.nic.in/

https://www.beeindia.gov.in/

https://morth.nic.in/

https://mnre.gov.in/en/

https://www.commerce.gov.in/

https://powermin.gov.in/

https://www.jalshakti-ddws.gov.in/

https://www.jalshakti-dowr.gov.in/offerings/schemes-and-services/details/namami-gange-AO5ATNtQWa

https://www.bis.gov.in/

https://www.oecd.org/en/data/indicators/environmental-tax.html

https://www.oecd.org/en/data/indicators/environmental-tax.html

Environmental taxes – A statistical guide 2024 edition Eurostat

https://cerclex.com/blog/from-a-linear-to-a-circular-economy-the-evolution-of-waste-management/

Environmental Policy in India by Debajit N. Sarkar

https://www.pib.gov.in/PressReleasePage.aspx?PRID=1705772&reg=3&lang=2

https://niti.gov.in/whats-new/advancing-circular-economy-waste-electronic-and-electrical-equipment-e-waste-and-lithium

https://mohua.gov.in/pdf/627b8318adf18Circular-Economy-in-waste-management-FINAL.pdf

https://sbmurban.org/storage/app/media/3R-Info-Booklet.pdf

Secretariat of the Basel Convention (1989) Basel convention on the control of trans boundary movements of hazardous wastes and their disposal. (https://www.basel.int/the-convention)

Secretariat of the Convention on Biological Diversity (SCBD) (1992) Convention on Biological Diversity (https://www.cbd.int/convention/)

https://mnre.gov.in/en/solar-schemes/

https://www.pib.gov.in/Pressreleaseshare.aspx?PRID=1692228&reg=3&lang=2

www.journalpressindia.com/siteadmin/upload_paper/1700465063_2_Importance%20and%20Relevance%20of%20Circular_Sunil%20B.%20Kapadia.pdf

https://doe.gov.in/files/circulars_document/NCEF_Brief_post_BE_2017_18.pdf

United Nations Environment Programme (UNEP) (2022) UNEP at a Glance (https://www.unep.org/about-un-environment/unep-glance)

United Nations Framework Convention on Climate Change (UNFCCC) (2015) Agreement (https://unfccc.int/process-and-meetings/the-paris-agreement/the-paris-agreement)

United States Environmental Protection Agency (USEPA) (2021) Clean Water Act. (https://www.epa.gov/laws-regulations/summary-clean-water-act)

Market-based instruments and sustainable innovation:A systematic literature review and critique by Maryam Mazaheri, Jaime Bonnin Roca, Arjan Markus, Bob Walrave. (https://www.sciencedirect.com/science/article/pii/S0959652622035193)

https://scholar.law.colorado.edu/cgi/viewcontent.cgi?article=1787&context=celj

Intergovernmental Fiscal Relations in India: Time for the Next Generation of Reforms by D.K. Srivastava, Madras School of Economics (Working Paper 222/2022)

Environment Policies in India by Abhay Kumar and Surjith Kartikeyan

(https://meta.eeb.org/2022/05/19/circular-economy-a-win-win-for-eu-india-cooperation-and-trade/)

https://ic-ce.com/icef-2022/

https://www.tyrestewardship.org.au/

https://tracanada.ca/end-of-life-tire-management/

https://www.tirestewardshipmb.ca/

https://www.tssk.ca/

https://unfccc.int/process-and-meetings/the-rio-conventions

https://www.clubofrome.org/

Andrew Leicester, Environmental taxes: economic principles and the UK experience

OECD Environmental Performance Reviews: United Kingdom2022

Circular Economy in Municipal Solid and Liquid Waste by Ministry of Housing and Urban Affairs, Government of India

Public policy and framework on environmental production and sustainable development in India: An overview by Dr. Kaushlendra Dixit in International Journal of Political Science and Governance

https://darpg.gov.in/sites/default/files/CSD-2023/Circular_Economyt.pdf#:~:text=Circularity%20in%20dry%20waste%20can,waste%20could%20also%20be%20included